IN THE
NEIGHBORHOODS

MARINA
RUSSIAN HILL
NORTH BEACH
CHINA-TOWN
PACIFIC HEIGHTS
NOB HILL
RICHMOND
WESTERN ADDITION
CIVIC CENTER
SOUTH OF MARKET
BUENA VISTA
EUREKA VALLEY
MISSION
POTRERO
SUNSET
NOE VALLEY
WEST OF TWIN PEAKS
BERNAL HEIGHTS
LAKE MERCED
EXCELSIOR
PORTOLA VALLEY
BAYVIEW
HUNTERS POINT
VISITACION VALLEY

Lombard
Broadway
Van Ness
Geary
Divisadero
Market
Haight
17th
Judah
Mission
Castro
Twin Peaks
7th
24th
Army
19th
Sunset
Taraval
Ocean
Third
Mansell

IN THE
NEIGHBORHOODS

A GUIDE TO THE JOYS AND DISCOVERIES
OF SAN FRANCISCO'S NEIGHBORHOODS

Susan Shepard

PHOTOGRAPHS BY
Gregg Mancuso

CHRONICLE BOOKS
San Francisco

Copyright © 1981 by Susan Shepard and Gregg Mancuso.
All rights reserved.
Printed in the United States of America.

Library of Congress Cataloging in Publication Data

Shepard, Susan.
    In the neighborhoods.

    1. San Francisco (Calif.)—Social life
and customs. 2. San Francisco (Calif.)—
History. 3. San Francisco (Calif.)—Descrip-
tion—Guide books. I. Title.
F869.S357S53   979.4'61   81-6154
ISBN 0-87701-144-3   AACR2

Book and cover design by Paula Schlosser.
Editing by Suzanne Lipsett.
Composition by Communi-Comp.

Chronicle Books
870 Market Street
San Francisco, CA 94102

CONTENTS

PREFACE

1 CHINATOWN 1

2 NORTH BEACH 13

3 NOB HILL • RUSSIAN HILL 25

4 CIVIC CENTER • THE TENDERLOIN 35

5 WESTERN ADDITION 41

6 PACIFIC HEIGHTS • THE MARINA • COW HOLLOW 47

7 THE RICHMOND 55

8 SOUTH OF MARKET • POTRERO HILL 61

9 DEATH OF AN OLD NEIGHBORHOOD 67

10 THE MISSION • BERNAL HEIGHTS 71

11 THE BAYSHORE 79

      PORTOLA • EXCELSIOR • VISITACION VALLEY
      CROCKER-AMAZON • BAYVIEW-HUNTERS POINT

12 EUREKA VALLEY • NOE VALLEY 83

13 BUENA VISTA 89

14 TWIN PEAKS • DIAMOND HEIGHTS • POINTS WEST 97

      ST. FRANCIS WOOD • INGLESIDE • OCEANVIEW
      MERCED HEIGHTS • WESTWOOD

15 THE SUNSET • LAKE MERCED 103

PREFACE

IT WAS ALMOST A HUNDRED years ago that Rudyard Kipling wrote, "San Francisco is a mad city, inhabited for the most part by perfectly insane people." Robert Wuthnow, a Berkeley sociologist, ventured a cautious explanation for this phenomenon: "The Bay Area lacks ultraconservative politics and strict devotion to established religions." From Emperor Norton down through the Monkey Block Gang, the Beats, the Flower Children, the Cockettes, the Symbionese Liberation Army, and the People's Temple, San Francisco has spawned both high-minded and perverse eccentrics as well as iconoclastic movements.

I certainly cannot explain why "strange things grow up out there," as Congressman Leo Ryan's mother said, but I have tried to show the individuality and character that shapes the various neighborhoods where San Franciscans live. Is San Francisco really a "mad city" to someone who lives in a quiet apartment at Lake Merced? Can anyone who's observed a Russian Orthodox Easter mass believe that the city suffers a "lack of strict religious devotion"?

Contrary to what visitors and some residents might think, all San Franciscans do not live in Victorians atop landscaped hills overlooking Angel Island. Many, in fact, live in stucco bungalows on flat, sun-baked or fog-shrouded streets. They all have their own neighborhood shops, hang-outs, and individual histories. Almost all San Franciscans I spoke to, no matter what part of the city they lived in, told me that their neighborhoods were convenient. "Convenient to what?" I asked. "Well, convenient to the things I like in my neighborhood." Exactly.

I hope this book serves as a general guide to some of the "conveniences" residents enjoy in their neighborhoods. It doesn't pretend to cover all the subneighborhoods, or to mark the precise borders between, say, Hayes Valley and the Haight-Fillmore, if true borders even exist. My intention was not to produce a planning department study.

My experiences, and those of photographer Gregg Mancuso, in the neighborhoods of San Francisco were shaped by the people we met, the bookstores we browsed in, the lunches we ate. I've tried to explain, with the help of the excellent statistical charts of The Coro Foundation's *District Handbook*, how each neighborhood came to be, who lives there and why, what to expect, and what not to miss. But to feel the neighborhood, you must go there yourself. *In the Neighborhoods* is meant to point the way.

S.S.
March 1981

To Robert Levering and Chuck

Neon and bright lights attract tourists to Chinatown's Grant Avenue.

1

CHINATOWN

To MOST CHINATOWN TOURISTS, Grant Avenue satisfies all the requirements for an authentic Chinese community. A suitably Chinese gate stands at the corner of Bush Street and Grant Avenue. China-fied buildings line the narrow street jammed with delivery trucks, Chinese residents, and more tourists. Cheap merchandise spills out of stores onto the sidewalks: fans from Taiwan, tin toys from Japan, and kung fu shoes from Hong Kong. More exclusive shops advertise "Number One Jade" and silk brocade. Even the phone booths are topped with pagoda like designs.

After passing through about six blocks of the Grant Avenue hoopla, the tourist can walk down to the Chinese Cultural Center, housed in the ugly high-rise Holiday Inn on Portsmouth Square, to see an exhibit on Chinese life and history. Typically, the tourist then heads back to a hotel, content that he or she has "done" Chinatown in but a few hours.

What this visitor will have seen is the *Sang Yee Gah*, the commercial street front, completely missing the *Gee Gah*, the upper-floor residences of the land-starved community, the back alleys crammed with herb shops and benevolent societies, and the hubbub of *Du Pon Gai* (an old Chinese name for Grant Avenue), where housewives shop for fresh duck and moon cakes. For despite Chinatown's position as a tourist center in the shadow of the downtown skyscrapers, this neighborhood could well be the most insular, conservative, and isolated community in the city.

San Francisco's Chinatown is the largest Chinese community on the West Coast, and the second largest Chinatown in the country (New York City's Chinese population surpassed San Francisco's in the early 1970s). Most of the city's 60,000 Chinese cluster in Chinatown, which makes this neighborhood more crowded than any urban area in the United States

outside Manhattan. A worker at Chinatown Neighborhood Improvement discussed with me the over-
crowding, lack of housing, garbage problems, and
flight of middle-class Chinese to the suburbs. But
when I asked why she remained in Chinatown, she
was surprised. "Why, you can get whatever you want
here; good food, fun, anything."

Three years ago, Alex Ching sold the Grant
Avenue jade shop he had owned for more than thirty
years. He now volunteers at the Chinese Historical
Society, at 17 Adler Alley, while he observes the
changing times in Chinatown. I quoted to him some
statistics: more than a third of Chinatown's residents
earn between $4,000 and $10,000 a year and have less
than a high school education, almost one-quarter of
the residents are over 60 years old. In return, he
described to me the Chinese immigrants who work
twelve hours a day, six days a week, in restaurants and
sewing sweat shops. "They never even make mini-
mum wage, but they can't speak English. What else
can they do?"

Ching remembers the 1950s exodus to the
Richmond, Sunset, and the Peninsula after a ban was
lifted on Chinese ownership of land outside Chinatown. He recalls the new influx of Chinese immigrants in the 1960s when the last of the exclusionary
immigration laws were dropped. He describes how
Stockton Street became the neighborhood's main
street as the tourist trade took over Grant.

Ching stays in Chinatown with his wife and four
children because it's his home—his friends and
traditions are there. He's proud of his children's
accomplishments: a daughter who's both an engineer
and an accomplished pianist, a son in law school,
another planning to follow his brother. He chuckles
over his youngest son's refusal to attend the afternoon

For many Chinatown children, after school there is more
school. These children attend an afternoon Chinese school on
Stockton Street where they learn Chinese culture
and calligraphy.

Chinese school to learn calligraphy; he prefers to play
baseball after English school. They all live at home.
"And believe me, I know where they are every minute.
The youth killings at the Golden Dragon in 1977
scared us all here."

Alex Ching represents the old school in Chinatown, the people who believe in education and financial success. This sector includes the leadership of the elders of the Chinese Six Companies, the traditional arbiter in community conflicts, founded in 1862. The younger generation sees their neighborhood, however colorful it may be, as a slum. They are turning to political activism to combat the poverty, outside land speculation, and the discrimination they consider the legacy of the Chinese in America.

In earlier days, the Chinese optimistically called California *Gam Saan*, the Golden Mountain, but what they too often found here was racism, violence, ghetto dwellings, and discriminatory laws. When the first three Chinese immigrants arrived in San Francisco on the American brig *Eagle* in 1848, what they found was a small community until recently called Yerba Buena, huddled around Portsmouth Square, the heart of the community then and of Chinatown now. Captain John B. Montgomery had planted the American flag from his ship, the *Portsmouth*, on the square just two years earlier. Already the area had passed from the domain of Costanoan Indians, to Spanish, then Mexican, and finally American rule, much to the dismay of one Sam Brannan, a Mormon who had fled to California to escape persecution in the United States.

In 1847, the year Yerba Buena was renamed San Francisco, the town got its first newspaper, Brannan's *California Star*. It was the *Star* that in 1848 announced the news that changed San Francisco overnight from a pueblo backwater into a true city—gold had been found in the American River a few hundred miles northeast from San Francisco. Along with the crews who jumped ship, the fortune-hunters from every country, the whores, the criminals, and the adven-

Chinese housewives shop almost daily at half-a-dozen stores. This young mother stops at an open-air produce stand to buy fruit.

turers, came the Cantonese, who fled famine and the Opium War in the Swangtung Province of southern China. In January 1850, 789 Chinese men and two Chinese women landed in San Francisco. By the end of the year, the Chinese population had risen to 4,018 men and 7 women, among whom was the soon-to-be notorious prostitute, Ah Toy, a madam "blooming with youth, beauty, and rouge," according to the *Alta California* in 1851.

The Chinese settled on Sacramento Street between Kearny and Dupont (now Grant) and soon displaced the establishments of the French hookers with Chinese shops, restaurants, and a newspaper in what became known as Little Canton, or Little China. Brothels, saloons, and gambling dens ringed Portsmouth Square. Vigilantes tried to keep the peace by hanging a number of offenders on or near the square. Chinese coolies (a word for laborer taken from the Chinese word for bitter toil, *ku li*), with their long queues and traditional dress, were tolerated during the boom days of the 1850s and 60s, when they worked the mines and built the transcontinental railroad (and later the Delta levees and Napa vineyards). But as soon as the work dried up in the inevitable crash of 1873, white San Franciscans saw Chinatown as Rudyard Kipling did: "A ward of the city of Canton set down in the most eligible business quarter of the city."

Gangs of unemployed whites tried to burn and beat the Chinese out of town. They humiliated Chinese men by cutting off their queues. They held anticoolie conventions on the barren sandlots of the city. In 1882, the government succumbed to the "yellow peril" hysteria with the Chinese Exclusion Act. America would take your tired, your poor, your hungry, but only if their eyes weren't slanted.

The associations, or tongs, that the Chinese established for protection and to procure justice for themselves backfired into gang warfare. These societies ran the opium trade, extortion rings, and assassination squads, which were known as hatchet-men for obvious reasons. The tongs imported young slave girls from China to serve as prostitutes. The girls were imprisoned in Chinatown basements, forced to take on all comers, and left to starve to death if they became ill or diseased. The Donaldina Cameron House, at 920 Sacramento, bears the name of the woman who, from 1895 to 1937, saved dozens of slave girls. The girls called her *Lo Mo*, Little Mother, but the whoremasters named her the Fahn Quai, White Devil. By 1926, according to Jerry Flamm's book, *Good Life in Hard Times*, a tough Irish cop named Jack Manion had finally flushed the fighting tongs off the streets of Chinatown.

One of the deadliest streets in Chinatown in the 1890s was Waverly Place, home of Chinese gangster Little Pete. Some sixty persons died in a seven-year war Pete initiated. To everyone's relief, in 1897 he was assassinated, while having his queue dressed. Waverly Place kept its reputation into the 1920s, when Dashiell Hammet mentioned it in his detective story "Dead Yellow Women." Today the alley shelters benevolent societies and the beautiful Tien How Temple, a Buddhist/Taoist/Confucianist joss house established at 125 Waverly more than a hundred years ago. Just follow the pungent smell of incense (the joss sticks, so named from a corruption of the Portuguese word for God, *Dios*) up to the fourth floor, all the nearer to heaven.

The year Little Pete died, four hundred laundries were run in Chinatown by law-abiding Chinese. The *San Francisco Reports of 1897* recorded that fifty Chinese were arrested that year for sleeping under ironing boards, smoking opium in laundries, or spraying clothing by spitting water on them. The plumbing inspector noted that "unclean disease breeding basements, saturated and littered with

An elderly gentleman strolls along Stockton Street. Almost
one quarter of Chinatown's residents are more than 60 years old.

Sappy romances and violent martial-arts movies screen at one
of six Chinese-language theaters in Chinatown. Sun Sing on
Grant broadcasts movie soundtracks on outdoor loudspeakers.

refuse, were the sleeping rooms of hundreds of Chinese. Apartments used for sleeping and working were foul with noxious odors and the accumulation of filth.''

The great earthquake and fire of 1906 totally destroyed Chinatown, and the city supervisors moved to relocate the Chinese to some less valuable piece of property. But the Chinese rebuilt and reinhabited their district before the City Hall bureaucracy could creak into action. The new buildings of Chinatown were built in the same style as the other Edwardian structures going up around the city. The Chinese added what some architects call "Chinoiserie" to their buildings in the 1920s, when white visitors began to tour Chinatown, much as curious whites began to go "slumming" in Harlem at around the same time. The rebuilt Chinatown was just as crowded as the old Chinatown, since it occupied the same blocks, between Stockton and Kearny, Broadway and Bush. By World War II, within Chinatown's confines an average of twenty persons shared a bath and twelve persons shared a kitchen.

Despite the significant migration to the suburbs in the 1950s and the construction of the Ping Yuen housing project in 1961, Chinatown currently is spilling over into the Russian and Nob Hill areas as well as into North Beach and the Civic Center. Along with Portsmouth Square, every tiny concrete playground and schoolyard teems with children and old men gambling at checkers and Mah Jongg.

On Sundays, the Chinese suburbanites journey back to Chinatown to buy pastries and visit with friends on the above-street balconies. Chinatown is their neighborhood even though they no longer live there. Chinatown functions as more than a neighborhood; it is the repository of a Chinese way of life that no longer exists in The People's Republic of China.

Chinatown is now struggling to absorb the latest wave of immigrants, ethnic Chinese refugees from Vietnam. These newcomers find it difficult to adjust to the strange ways and dialects of Chinese Americans. More than three-quarters of Chinatown's residents are foreign born.

The conflict continues between the conservative older generation and the Americanized younger people. But for every Chinese American who would rather play baseball than learn Chinese calligraphy there is a young Chinese American who fights to save the Chinese immigrant poetry on the immigration barracks walls at Angel Island, which stands as a monument to the Chinese presence in America.

A DAY IN CHINATOWN

Christmastime is one of my favorite times of the year to wander through Chinatown. The stores on Grant Avenue are a treasure trove of such stocking stuffers as kung fu movie posters, bizarre space toys, delicate rice bowls, and cheap gags. The Shanghai and the Bargain Bazaar, side by side at 645 and 667 Grant, carry a good selection of fun junk.

I also look to Grant Avenue for some unique and beautiful gifts. Filia, at 437 Grant, is the place to go for silk brush paintings and cloths embroidered in gold thread. Check the baskets filled with coral, jade, and pearls at this store. Sometimes they sell very old jade bangles cheaply if they have a slight crack. Be sure to examine the incredibly ornate sequined jackets and skirts in the rear of the store. None go for less than $300, but the workmanship is exquisite. Hip Ling, farther up Grant, features a large selection of silk shirts with plain or mandarin collars. The Chinese favor the blouses with the delicate filigree around the neck.

I once bought a complicated kite at the Chinatown Kite Shop (717 Grant) after the saleswoman assured me her child of four put one together easily. It took me three days. Better buy the simple Chinese kites with colorful bird or animal heads. They sell here for less than $2.

The jumpiest time of the year in Chinatown is the New Year season (set astrologically, but usually falling in February). Even the two year olds are armed with firecrackers, which they delight in exploding at your feet, especially when you're talking in a phone booth. The firecrackers, red paper signs (for good luck), lion dancers, and strange refrains of the Chinese Opera drifting down from balcony stereos make the neighborhood even more fascinating than usual. My advice is to skip the three-hour-long parade (impossible to see over the heads of three rows of curbside spectators). You can see what the parade's dragon looks like by examining the dragon in the lobby of 838 Grant.

Chinese New Year is the perfect time to bone up on Chinese American history at the tiny Historical Society (17 Adler Place) or the Chinese Cultural Center (third floor of the Holiday Inn at 750 Kearny). The Cultural Center has had exhibits ranging from peasant art of mainland China to the history of anti-Chinese sentiment in California. The staff can tell you where and when performances of the Chinese Opera can be seen. The opera used to be performed regularly, but now you can see this unusual blend of music, mime, martial arts, acrobatics, and acting only during New Year festivities. I frequently buy intricate paper cut-outs and posters at the Cultural Center store, where also available are copies of the locally published *Island*, a book of the poetry that Chinese immigrants wrote on the walls of their barracks at Angel Island.

The Chingwah Lee Art Studio, at 9 Old Chinatown Lane, contains a collection of fine Oriental art. Another kind of display is on view at the Chinatown Wax Museum (601 Grant). Don't pay money to see the interior of the museum, but take a few minutes to peer in the window at the jars of dead animals and snakes. Some of the herb shops also sport these kinds of curiosities. Ellison Enterprise (802 Stockton) is a good one.

Sappy romance and wild martial-arts movies show at six Chinese-language theaters in the area. A bunch of schoolchildren is always clustered out in front of Sun Sing (1021 Grant) listening to the movies over the outdoor loudspeakers. The children of the neighborhood overrun Portsmouth Square during the New Year carnival, when a Ferris wheel and other rides take over the park. The park is so crowded then that people completely cover the monument to Robert Louis Stevenson. More than a hundred years ago, when he lived at 608 Bush Street, Stevenson spent hours writing in Portsmouth Square. His recollections of the neighborhood are to be found in *The Wreckers*.

What's a holiday without food—especially in Chinatown? Some chefs insist that the two greatest cuisines in the world are French and Chinese.

Chinese building ornamentation, like the decoration on this bank, began to appear in the 1920s. The unadorned building facades of Commercial Street illustrate Chinatown's 19th century style.

Chinese cooking has been popular in California since 1848, when the Canton Restaurant opened its doors on the corner of Jackson and Kearny Streets. In recent years, the spicier cooking of inland China has pleased the palate at such restaurants as Hunan (make sure you go to the original cramped Hunan at 853 Kearny) and Shanghai Winter Garden (631 Broadway). *Dim Sum*, the steamed pastries stuffed with meats or vegetables that you choose and pay for individually, are perfect for lunch at Asia Garden (772 Pacific) or the Hong Kong Tea House (835 Pacific). You can take out great *dim sum* at the Yong Kee Rice Noodle Shop (732 Jackson).

The best way to eat Chinese food is to shop for it the way the locals do, at half a dozen different stores.

The Dupont Market retains Grant Avenue's original name (some of the old-timers still call Grant *Du Pon Gai*), where the large store occupies number 1100. The fish and meat market displays pig snouts, live crab and carp, squid, and fresh prawns, along with the usual chicken and beef. Most stores have a few Peking roast ducks hanging neck-down in the window, but why not buy yours at the take-out section of the notorious Golden Dragon (157 Waverly Place). Finish your meal with a moon cake from the Kay Wah Pastry Company (1039 Stockton).

Drinking in Chinatown should be done at the stodgy, faded-class Empress of China (838 Grant), or the oddball Li Po (916 Grant), a bar complete with Buddha and moon gate.

Crowds of Chinese men gather daily in Portsmouth Square to gamble on checkers, dominoes, cards, or mah jongg.

No matter what San Francisco cabbies tell you, Coit Tower on Telegraph
Hill was not designed to resemble a fireplug. The tower presides over
the activity of North Beach residents in Washington Square.

2

NORTH BEACH

ITALIANS, BASQUES, CHINESE, old Beats, young punks, strip-joint barkers, female impersonators, exotic dancers from the He/She Love Acts, interior decorators, architects, the avant-trendy and the apres-bummy—they're all to be found in North Beach.

This neighborhood, named for a beach that was land-filled in the 1800s, nestles diagonally north from the financial district between Russian and Telegraph Hills. Although it's a small area geographically, many people believe North Beach and San Francisco are synonymous. An article in the *New York Times* even identified it (ignorantly rather than facetiously) as North Beach, California.

At the corner of Broadway and Columbus Avenue, North Beach dazzles tourists with neon and the flashing red-lightbulb nipples on the Condor's Carol Doda sign. Hurrying to catch the drag queens at Finocchio's, the tourists barely notice the few signposts of 1950s beat culture still extant on Columbus: City Lights Bookstore and two bars,

Spec's and Vesuvio's. Above the din of traffic one hears jazz, New Wave, blues, rock, reggae, and jukebox opera.

At the end of Columbus Avenue, at Fisherman's Wharf, is another kind of nightlife. The pinball arcades, wax museum, t-shirt shops, and motels have pushed the few real fishermen back behind Jefferson Street between Jones and Leavenworth. Up Fish Alley, one block removed from what a fisherman calls "one big Disneyland," the tourists disappear, the boats look funky and used, and the corrugated metal and clapboard warehouses that line the old wooden wharf house, not redwood burl tables and cypress knee lamps offered for sale, but rather factories processing fresh fish caught in the bay.

Looking out from the lagoon, you'll see the old paddle-wheeler *Eureka* tied up at the Hyde Street Pier with the other historic ships that make up the Maritime State Historic Monument. The fishing boats have been motorized and equipped with radar for years, but somehow this spot seems unchanged from the turn-of-the-century days, when the wharf, lined with lateen-rigged Italian feluccas, was known as Italy Harbor.

My companion on the dock, John, informs me that in fact everything is very different now. The shrimp and oyster are all fished out, for one thing. John remembers when "fishermen used to come in with decks crawling with crabs. They'd crawl right off the boat and no one cared, because there were so many. It's not so easy finding crab now."

The old-timers who die out aren't being replaced by their sons and daughters (there are about five women fishing out of the area) at a rate that would keep the old breed alive. The old Sicilian fishermen like Joe Torrente, a seventy-two year old recently lost in the bay along with his son, are the last of their kind in North Beach.

Fisherman's Wharf is not the only place the Italians are leaving. They've been migrating to the suburbs from North Beach and Telegraph Hill since World War II, while the Chinese and young professionals quickly take their place.

Captain Pietro Bonzi and his son Orazio were the first Italians to arrive in San Francisco in 1840. By 1900, the Italians had displaced the Irish from Telegraph Hill and outnumbered other minority groups. The Irish themselves had overrun Telegraph Hill's first residents, the Chilean prostitutes who set up tents on the hill to cater to the desires of the Forty-Niners.

Telegraph Hill looked quite different during the Gold Rush. Although the height of the hill is the same (284 feet), the east slope was once smooth and round and covered with goats. The barren, jagged cliff we see now was created by sailors digging out ballast for their empty ships' holds back in the days when lagoons lapped at the hill's base. The hill had already gone through at least three names by the time of the Gold Rush (Loma Alta, Windmill, and Signal), but the Morse Code signal station set up on the hill in 1853 contributed the name that stuck.

Little Chile, on the west slope of the hill, endured violent attacks from the lawless band of cutthroats and thieves who lived in Sydneytown, on the south side of the hill. These "Sydney Ducks" pillaged the Chileans with the war cry, "California for Californians," an ironic slogan, since the Ducks were mostly Australian ticket-of-leave convicts.

The thugs and hoodlums (a word coined in San Francisco at the time) of Sydneytown gained a worldwide reputation for their viciousness. The area was renamed the Barbary Coast after the equally terrifying North African pirate haven. Every whore, pimp, pickpocket, opium addict, and murderer gathered here along with the sailors who were often drugged with Mickey Finns (another San Francisco invention) and spirited off as deckhands on some undermanned hell ship. This practice was known as shanghaiing, yet another San Francisco addition to the dictionary. The theaters of the area featured live acts involving women and horses (or other animals). Despite the efforts of the Vigilance Committees of the 1850s, the Barbary Coast partied on until antiopium laws and the Red Light Abatement Act of 1917 finally closed down the coast after World War I.

The old Barbary Coast area between Montgomery, Pacific, Washington, and Kearny is now known as Jackson Square, the first district to be designated an historic site in the city. In the 1950s, interior decorators renovated the old three-story buildings, exposing their brick walls. The area now

The apartments on Upper Grant Avenue illustrate San Francisco's
passion for bay windows, even when there's no bay view.

houses the offices of architects, lawyers (Melvin Belli's office is one of the most dandified buildings), and designers. A grand group of 1850s buildings stands in the 700 block of Montgomery.

By the time the Italians took over Telegraph Hill in the 1890s, the Barbary Coast was already tame enough to be included as a tourist attraction. All that's left now of the original Spanish-speaking population is their church, Nuestra Senora de Guadaloupe, at 908 Broadway. The last goat was seen on the hill in 1925.

Thanks to a bucket brigade using barrels of home-made red wine, the Italians managed to save a number of old wooden cottages from the post-earthquake fire of 1906, which destroyed North Beach. But they couldn't save the hill from the moneyed classes in the 1930s. On the tails of the artists and bohemians who had begun living on the hill in the 1890s came well-to-do San Franciscans, who quickly pushed out the residents they found there. By 1935, an article in the *Chronicle* entitled "Bohemians Edged Out" told the story.

Today Telegraph Hill is the most sought after address in the city. Despite the steady stream of tourists that roars up the hill to admire the view and the wonderful WPA frescoes inside Coit Tower (designed by Civic Center architect Arthur Brown and named for Lillie Hitchcock Coit in 1933), Telegraph Hill is a quiet, almost rural neighborhood marked by pedestrian stairways and beautifully landscaped by one-time resident Grace Marchant. The houses on Filbert Street, Greenwich Street, Napier Lane, Calhoun Terrace, and Montgomery Street are small Victorian cottages, elegant 1930s Moderne buildings, or international-style apartment houses. Bay views, gardens, cats, and quiet—what more could a San Franciscan want?

Those other things—good food, lively cafes, music, entertainment, international shopping, and action—are right at the bottom of the hill in North Beach proper. To the tourist, the heart of North Beach is the great white way at Broadway and Columbus. But to the resident, it's Washington Square, in front of the white twin-towered Sts. Peter and Paul Roman Catholic Church.

Washington Square (which holds a statue not of George, but of Benjamin Franklin) is the main open space for the 13,000 or so residents of North Beach. The land was set aside as a park in 1847 and relandscaped in 1955. Chinese and Italian ladies and old men occupy the park benches (but never the same one), while winos, frisbee-throwers, and kids hang out on the grass. From the park you can catch a bus up Telegraph Hill or a cable car over Russian Hill to the wharf, or you can walk into the neighborhood.

Since North Beach burned down in 1906, few Victorian-style houses remain. Most of the neighborhood buildings are three-story, wood-frame, Edwardian-style structures, on narrow streets and even narrower alleys. North Beach has been a crowded, popular, and active area ever since the Gold Rush. The average resident is between the ages of 25 and 44, white, foreign-born, and a skilled laborer who rents an apartment. But statistics are grossly misleading in North Beach. The population is one-quarter college graduates and one-third Chinese. Italian and Chinese businesses meet and mix on Stockton near Vallejo, and on upper Grant.

The international reputation of "North Beach, California," however, is not due to Italians, Chinese, or

This unique moderne apartment starred in the Humphrey Bogart film *Dark Passage*. It stands beside the beautifully landscaped Filbert Steps on Telegraph Hill.

the pleasant park. The Beats of the 1950s put North Beach on the map. Jack Kerouac adapted the word *beat* from *beatitude* to describe cats like himself who rejected Eisenhower America for poetry, jazz, eastern philo-sophy, and wanderlust. He wrote *On the Road* in 1951-52 at his friend Neal Cassady's place at 29 Russell, an alley off Hyde between Union and Green.

During the 1950s, Beats congregated at Enrico Banducci's hungry i (for id), first in a basement at 149 Columbus, then in a bigger cellar at 599 Jackson (where the International Hotel stood before it was demolished in 1979). Here comedians Mort Sahl and Lenny Bruce played. They also hung out at Henri Lenoir's Vesuvio Bar, next door to City Lights Bookstore, and later at Spec's, across Columbus on Adler Alley. Lawrence Ferlinghetti opened the first all-paperback bookstore in 1953, and soon afterwards began publishing Beat writers.

Allen Ginsberg electrified the Beats when he read his poem "Howl" at the Six Gallery at 3119 Fillmore on October 13, 1955. The next year the beatniks (so named by Herb Caen) were splashed across America in *Life* magazine, when Ferlinghetti and other City Lights employees were arrested on obscenity charges for publishing "Howl."

The Beats became notorious. Just as the Barbary Coast died when it became a tourist attraction, so did the North Beach Beat scene. The Beats fought back at the bus tours of their neighborhood with a squaresville tour of Union Square (a hundred North Beachers paraded through the chic square to the beat of a bongo drum). But by the early 1960s, the Beat movement had died away, to be reborn in another form across town in the Haight a few years later. In his book, *Literary San Francisco*, Ferlinghetti quoted Henri Lenoir: "Then the topless boys took advantage of all the tourists looking for beatniks, and decided to give them sex." Carol Doda bared her breasts and danced at the Condor in 1964, and thus began the succession of topless

Molinari's is the best known Italian delicatessen in North Beach.
It smells even better than it looks.

college coeds, bottomless males, and the He/She love acts that have characterized Broadway ever since.

On other porno strips in other towns, everything but the flesh-peddlers is ultimately driven out. But Broadway never degenerated into a totally seamy red-light district. Legitimate theaters and clubs keep cropping up, including a new comedy club owned by Enrico Banducci, former owner of the old hungry i.

Fifties clothing is again appearing on the streets of North Beach, not on old Beats, but on young punk rockers who hang out at the New Wave clubs Mabuhay Gardens, and the Stone to hear the Dead Kennedys, Mutants, or Los Microwaves. The punks, in their tight black jeans, leopard-look tops, magenta-spiky hair, and catwoman shades, are just the latest in a long stream of bohemians to call North Beach home. Anything could be next.

TWENTY-FOUR HOURS IN "NORTH BEACH, CALIFORNIA"

You like architecture? A little poetry or history? Or would you rather stuff yourself full of eclairs and dance all night? Whatever strikes your fancy day or night can be found in North Beach, the most self-sufficient neighborhood in town.

Start your day at 4:30 A.M. down at Fish Alley (behind Jefferson at Jones). This is the only time the honky-tonk Fisherman's Wharf is quieter than the old wharf, where the fishing boats are gearing up for a day on the bay. Watch the dawn rise afterwards at Aquatic Park. You may even see some of the crazy swimmers from the nearby clubs braving the frigid waters. Every New Year's Day the Polar Bear Club swimmers take the plunge here. Stroll over to the west side of the Maritime Museum (Polk at Beach) to examine the bocce court. Later in the day, a group of Italian men will gather to argue and throw the bocce ball.

There's no problem with cable car queues at six A.M., when the cars start running. Hop a Powell-Mason car at Taylor and Bay, ride as far as Filbert and Mason, and walk a block to Washington Square for an omelette breakfast at Mama's (Stockton at O'Farrell). Now you're properly fortified to shop on upper Grant Avenue, above Columbus. Grant Avenue, originally called Calle de la Fundacion, is the oldest street in the city. The first private house in the city, that of Captain Richardson, stood on Grant. In June, a street fair is held on the upper part of Grant, but the street's hopping just about any time.

My favorite stores are the Shlock Shop (1418 Grant) and Poor Taste (1562 Grant) for outrageous old clothes, broken but beautiful pocket watches, and kitschy knickknacks. At the neon Sherwin-Williams "We cover the earth" sign is Figone's (1351 Grant), an old-time, wooden-floored hardware store where you can buy pasta machines. A block off Grant at Green, rest a moment in the pleasant garden behind the Old Spaghetti Factory (478 Green) before going into the Philippe Bonnafont Gallery. Bonnafont shows mostly architects' work in the gallery he converted from an old bocce court. The Museo-Italo-Americano (678 Green) shows the art of (obviously) Italian Americans. Buy a loaf of fine Italian bread at the Italian-French Baking Company (1501 Grant) as you wander past the Chinese markets and real estate offices that have lately moved onto Grant.

Out on Columbus, pick up some freshly roasted coffee (you can follow your nose) at Graffeo Coffee Roasting Company (733 Columbus). Stop in at the tres-punk Postcard Palace (756 Columbus) for some very untraditional, "wish-you-were-here" cards of the city.

For lunch, try an overstuffed Italian sandwich to go from either Molinari's (1373 Columbus) or Panelli Bros. (1419 Stockton) and eat it in Washington Square. Little Joe's (325 Columbus), Cafferata Ravioli Factory (700 Columbus), or Columbus (611 Broadway) are all good counter-service alternatives to a picnic lunch.

The best napoleons and eclairs (and don't forget the cream puffs) for dessert come from Stella's (446

Columbus) and Victoria's (1362 Stockton). Don't buy the cannoli. No one west of New York's Little Italy or Boston's North End seems to know that you never fill a cannoli shell with cheese until the customer buys it. If it's a Saturday afternoon, you must drink an after-lunch cappucino or espresso at Cafe Trieste (609 Vallejo), because the family-owners turn out to sing opera. The tiny Bohemian Cigar Company (1715 Union) is a slightly quieter spot, although I was driven out one day by a raucous rendition of "Santa Lucia."

You're as ready as you'll ever be to tackle Telegraph Hill by way of Filbert Street. The view and the murals in Coit Tower at the crest of the hill are worth a look, but continue down the Filbert and Greenwich steps to catch your breath surrounded by bay views and flowers. There's a very old Victorian cottage (c. 1855) at 9 Calhoun, and a 1939 building by famed Los Angeles architect Richard Neutra at 66 Calhoun, but I like the reddish house at the end of the street where the owners dangle sprinklers down the concrete walls to water the wildflowers.

Walk down the hill via Montgomery Street, past the old Barbary Coast, now Jackson Square, to the Transamerica Pyramid (600 Montgomery). A gallery in the building occasionally shows exhibits by or about North Beachers. They recently showed Vesuvio's owner Henri Lenoir's memorabilia from the 1940s through the 1970s. The pyramid stands on what used to be the Monkey Block, a building built in 1853 that became the hang-out of another group of bohemians, the writers George Sterling, Ambrose Bierce, Frank Norris, and Jack London. A Turkish bath in the basement owned by one Tom Sawyer was frequented by none other than Mark Twain (Sawyer and Twain played penny ante together). The writers ate in Pappa Coppa's restaurant and drank mind-blowing Pisco Punches at the Bank Exchange Bar. The 1906 fire spared the building but by then the bohemians moved elsewhere and the building was finally demolished in 1959. There's another Bank Exchange Bar in the Pyramid now that doesn't sell the same Pisco Punch, but they do serve free hors d'oeuvres.

If you're still thirsty after walking up Columbus, stop in for a glass of San Francisco's only native beer, Anchor Steam, at the Albatross (155 Columbus), Spec's (12 Adler Place), or Vesuvio's (255 Columbus). The Albatross is worth a visit just for its unusual antique fans attached in a row to a long pipe. Another bar in the area, Tosca's (242 Columbus), is best later in the evening, when the opera-only jukebox is going full blast.

City Lights Bookstore (261 Columbus) sits in the middle of these watering-holes. The bookstore has a good selection of paperbacks, but why not buy one of the one hundred titles City Lights itself has published? All copies of *Literary San Francisco* (Harper & Row) sold here are signed by coauthors Lawrence Ferlinghetti and Nancy J. Peters.

You've still got about eight hours to go in North Beach, so you'd better eat hearty. Homey Basque dinners are served family style at the Obrero (1208 Stockton) and Basque Hotels (15 Romolo Place). Good Italian, family-style meals are cooked at the New Pisa (550 Green) and La Pantera (1234 Grant). For more elegant Northern Italian cuisine try Il Giglio (545 Francisco). Basta Pasta (1268 Grant) and Caffe Sport (574 Green) offer good pasta-seafood combinations.

Plan the evening's entertainment over coffee and dessert at an open-air sidewalk cafe such as Enrico's

Amateur opera singers, usually relations of the proprietors,
entertain the capuccino and espresso crowd on Saturday
afternoons at the Caffe Trieste.

Telegraph Hill is in the heart of the city, but its pedestrian lanes,
like the Filbert Steps, are quiet and tree-shrouded. Residents gladly
park their cars below the hill to trek dozens of steps to their homes.

(504 Broadway) or the Savoy Tivoli (1438 Grant). The backrooms at both the Savoy and the Old Spaghetti Factory feature comedy, live music, or even Flamenco dance. Up for punk? The Mabuhay Gardens, or Fab Mab (443 Broadway), showcases local and national New Wave bands. For more traditional rock, check out Gulliver's (348 Columbus), or the ultra-sleazy 2232 Bar at 2232 Grant. Keystone Korner (750 Vallejo) and Cadell Place are two places to go for jazz, while the blues wails nightly at the Coffee Gallery (1353 Grant).

The Intersection, housed in an old church at 756 Union Street, specializes in old cartoons, poetry readings, and unusual theater. Other legitimate theater crops up here and there between the skin joints on Broadway—notably, the Phoenix (430 Broadway) and the Hippodrome (412 Broadway). The San Francisco-grown zany musical comedy *Beach Blanket Babylon Goes to the Stars* has been playing for years at the lovely old Club Fugazi (678 Green).

Most establishments close down at 2 A.M., but on weekends Mooney's Pub (1525 Grant) serves food twenty-four hours a day. Finish out the wee hours with Mooney's chow and then go to bed—you've just survived twenty-four hours in North Beach, California.

Poet George Sterling once looked down over his "cool grey city of love"
from the top of Russian Hill. The view today from Ina Coolbrith Park
is of the cold glass city of skyscrapers.

3

NOB HILL · RUSSIAN HILL

IN A CITY FAMOUS FOR HILLS, Nob Hill may be the most famous hill of all. The thousands of servicemen who shipped out of San Francisco to the Pacific during World War II still wax sentimental over the cable car ride and the Top of the Mark. Others remember the maudlin scene from the old Clark Gable/Jeannette MacDonald movie *San Francisco*, when the sweet old lady's Nob Hill mansion is dynamited during the fire of 1906. Today the same visitors who expect the Golden Gate Bridge to be gold express dismay over the lack of mansions on Nob Hill. Even San Franciscans dismiss the hill as "just a bunch of old hotels and a cathedral," as one native told me.

Despite the presence of such posh hotels as the Fairmont, the Mark Hopkins, and Stanford Court on the 376-foot-high summit, Nob Hill is home for more than 9,000 residents. Dave Vogel, the former president of Nob Hill Neighbors, points out that "millionaires live within a block of people on welfare," and it's true

that the rich nabobs (for whom the hill was named) no longer have the hill to themselves. During the 1960s, less prosperous Chinese from nearby Chinatown moved onto the north and west slopes near the heavily gay Polk Gulch shopping area.

But Nob Hill is still a bit more exclusive than your average city neighborhood. The hotels drip marble and crystal, the high-rise luxury apartment buildings ooze art deco elegance, and Huntington Park proudly displays a replica of the Tartarughe Fountain of Italy.

Unlike its wealthy neighbor, Russian Hill, the Hill of Golden Promise (Nob Hill's early name) started out as a home for the filthy rich, with the emphasis on the filthy. In 1856, when most wealthy San Franciscans lived on the more accessible Rincon Hill, dentist Arthur Hayne built Nob Hill's first structure where the Fairmont Hotel stands today. Hayne supposedly chose the steep, barren hill for his house to discourage late-night visits by toothache victims. A few other rich citizens—William Walton, William Coleman, and George Hearst—followed Hayne up the hill. Their cozy set-up ended in 1873, the year Andrew Hallidie successfully tested his cable cars on the Clay Street hill between Jones and Kearny. The next year Leland Stanford, president of the Central Pacific Railroad, formed the California Street Cable Railroad and in 1875 became the first railroad nabob to build on Nob Hill.

Stanford's railroad partners, the Big Four, quickly followed his lead. The extravagantly pretentious French Chateau, Italianate, and Gothic-style mansions of Charles Crocker, Leland Stanford, Mark Hopkins, and Collis Huntington were matched by the equally ostentatious mansions of Silver Kings James G. Fair and James Flood. Robert Louis Stevenson described Nob Hill as "a kind of slum, being the habitat of the mere millionaire. It is there that they gathered together, vying with each other in display."

The wealthy residents of Rincon Hill and South Park despised the nouveau riche of Nob Hill for their fabulous wealth and excesses (James Flood employed a servant to polish his $30,000 brass fence every day), but they soon deserted Rincon for the richer air of Nob Hill. Everyone else hated the Big Four for their greed and corruption.

The four had started out innocuously enough, charging Forty-Niners high prices for necessities in their drygoods stores in Sacramento. The four saw their chance to make a monumental fortune when they met Theodore Judah, an engineer who dreamed of connecting the east and west coasts with a railroad. The four feigned indifference to Judah's plan while he spent years trying to convince Congress of the railroad's worth. In 1862, fears of the Confederates

taking over California persuaded Congress to give the railroad builders free use of public lands along the route, as well as $16,000 a mile for construction through low lands and three times that amount for tracks through mountainous terrain.

The Big Four suddenly became very interested in railroads, and Judah soon found himself locked out of his own plan with a payoff of $100,000. The four changed Judah's route maps to include more hill country (for the higher subsidy) and hired Irish and Chinese immigrants to slave away on the tracks. The construction of the Central Pacific Railroad began in 1863 and ended six arduous years later.

The mammoth fortune of the Big Four went on to fund the Nob Hill mansions, Stanford University, the Huntington Library in Pasadena, land for Huntington Park and Grace Cathedral, Leland Stanford's successful campaigns for governor of California (1885-1893), and all the payoffs, kick-backs, and bribes the four contributed to politicians (as revealed in the correspondence between Huntington and lawyer David Colton in a notorious court case).

The Big Four's ugly Nob Hill monuments to Mammon blew up or burned down in the 1906 earthquake-fire, to the satisfaction of many a citizen. Ironically, the only two buildings left standing belonged to Silver Kings: James Flood's brownstone mansion (the one with the brass fence, now owned by the very stuffy Pacific Union Club); and the shell of the Fairmont Hotel, built in James Fair's memory by his daughter Tessie Oelrichs.

Fair and Flood, like the Big Four, got their first break during the Gold Rush, but as miners rather than shopkeepers. Back in San Francisco, the two opened a saloon in the financial district where they

Silver King James Flood once employed a servant to polish his $30,000
brass fence every day. The ultra stuffy and strictly male Pacific Union
Club now occupies the Nob Hill mansion with the badly tarnished fence.

picked up stock tips from their customers. They swapped bartending for stockbrokering until they teamed up with fellow Dubliners (actually, Flood's parents hailed from Ireland, whereas he came from New York) John Mackay and William O'Brien and hit it rich in the Nevada silver mines. The consoli- dated Virginia mine alone yielded $230,000,000. Fair, like Stanford and Hearst, bought himself a political post, that of United States Senator, where he distinguished himself as the first Senator to be sued for adultery. He settled the case with his ex-wife for $5,000,000.

A lone figure prays in Grace Cathedral on Nob Hill. Almost
40 years were required to complete the concrete Gothic church.

Nob Hill calmed down after the Big Four, the Silver Kings, and the 1906 earthquake. The hill was rebuilt with Edwardian flats (like the group on Taylor near Sacramento) with a few hotels. The first wave of luxury high-rises hit the hill in the 1920s. In 1928, a thirty-seven-year-long construction job began, the building of Grace Cathedral on the site of the Crocker mansion. A second wave of high-rise apartments spread over both Nob and Russian Hills in the 1960s. During the next decade, the neighborhoods adopted building-height limitations and nervously experienced a new threat, serious to areas where 88 percent of the residents are renters: condominium conversions.

In 1980, comedian James Wesley Fox joked about the remedy for a blackout on Nob Hill. "There's a cop making him get in his car and drive away." But the predominantly white tourist population obscures the fact that one-fifth of Nob Hill's residents are nonwhite. Single adults make up half of the neighborhood, the highest percentage of singles in any area of the city. More than half the residents walk to work in nearby Chinatown, Polk Gulch, or the financial district—a convenience that many cite as the reason they came to the area in the first place.

For a ritzy Thursday evening, follow the footsteps of the residents and walk Nob Hill. Grace Cathedral, the city's major Episcopal church, offers a lovely evensong (sung prayers) every Thursday at 5:30 P.M. Notice the church's beautiful golden doors; they are casts of the Ghiberti Doors on the Baptistry in Florence. After evensong, walk to the Big Four Bar (1075 California) and ruminate over the rewards of the ill-gotten gains of the four for whom this place is named. The bar looks like something out of a private dining car on the Central Pacific Railroad, with leather chairs, a brass bar, and wood panelling. Move over to L'Etoile, also in the Huntington Hotel, where the pianist, Peter Mintun, plays the Cole Porter and Gershwin tunes that recall Nob Hill's rebirth in the twenties, thirties, and forties.

The Top of the Mark was remodeled in a tacky style years ago and the Fairmont Crown Room is not much better. Still, if you must have a Nob Hill view, the Fairmont does have a grand lobby designed by Stanford White, as well as an exhilarating glass-sided exterior elevator.

Walk or ride a cable car to another kind of world at the foot of California Street at Polk. On your way there you'll notice more of those small Edwardian-style apartment houses. The commercial strip, called Polk Gulch, developed as a shopping area for both Nob and Russian Hills. Now it is just about half white and half Chinese, but the gay men of the area make up the most visible group. The southern part of Polk Gulch used to be known as Polk Strasse, for its large population of German merchants, whose shops were wiped out in the 1906 fire. They rebuilt the street only to be forced out during the Great Depression by hotels and businesses. The German National Community Hall, built by German residents in 1910, became California Hall (625 Polk), home of such events as the Exotic-Erotic New Year's Eve Ball.

Gays started moving into the old neighborhood in the 1950s, and by the 1970s many Polk Street businesses, like the Palms Cafe (1406 Polk), Polk Gulch Saloon (1092 Post), and Hard On Leather (1133 Polk) catered to a largely gay clientele. Hundreds of gay men paraded down the street in drag on Halloween, until violence ended the event in 1979, or promenaded on Polk in July during the annual street fair.

The center of gay life has moved to Castro Street in recent years, and now Polk Gulch businesses serve, besides gays, Asians, office workers, and residents of Nob and Russian Hills.

A few blocks east up the hill from Polk and north of Nob Hill sits a neighborhood that *A Guide to Architecture in San Francisco and Northern California* describes as "epitomizing that peculiarly San Francisco paradox of upper class unpretentiousness: Russian Hill." For a hill 294 feet high, Russian Hill manages to maintain a low profile. Unlike Nob Hill, with its high concentration of commercial land (more than half), Russian Hill harbors almost no restaurants, shops, or hotels on its quiet streets to lure outsiders to the neighborhood. Looking up the hill from North Beach, the casual passerby might conclude, incorrectly, that Russian Hill's summit holds only high-rise apartment houses. Between those high-rises and above the lower slopes full of three-story flats nestle countrylike pedestrian lanes and parks, spectacular views, and some of the oldest and most architecturally interesting houses in the city.

Russian Hill has cultivated an image of being off the beaten track for as long as Nob Hill has pushed its Midas-touch myth. Like Telegraph Hill, Russian Hill's steep sides deterred all but goats and poor people from settling on its wild, mustard-covered slopes, where legend has it that Russian seal hunters were buried. The city's first execution took place on Russian Hill when Jose Forni was hanged in 1852. That year, William Penn Humphries, an old Indian fighter, built the first real house on the hill, at

Chinese families are expanding beyond Chinatown to the north and west slopes of Nob Hill, near Polk Gulch.

Chestnut and Hyde. The Fusier House, one of only two octagon houses now left in San Francisco, went up five years later at 1067 Green.

While some well-to-do San Franciscans built fine houses on Russian Hill, a small black community grew up briefly on the southwest slopes during the 1870s. The hill entered its most notorious period in the 1890s, when the city's bohemian intelligentsia took up residence. From the heights of Russian Hill, poet George Sterling looked down over his "cool grey city of love" along with writers Will and Wallace Irwin, Gelett Burgess, Charles Norris, Charles Caldwell Dobie, and John Dewey, and artists Maynard Dixon, William Kuth, and Douglas Tilden. Ina Coolbrith, California's first poet laureate, drew these and other writers to her literary salon on Russian Hill. Mark Twain, Bret Harte, Ambrose Bierce, and Joaquin Miller paid frequent visits to Coolbrith's house. As an Oakland librarian, Coolbrith personally selected books for the young Isadora Duncan and Jack London to read. Her name is remembered in a small, lovely park on Taylor between Fallon and Green Streets. A larger, more active park at the top of the wiggly block of Lombard Street commemorates George Sterling.

While the literary lights were meeting on Russian Hill, one of the city's most famous architects, Willis Polk, was developing the summit of Vallejo Street for the Livermore family. Before the 1906 fire, Polk designed or remodeled houses at 1013–15–17 (where Polk himself lived), 1019, 1034, 1036, and 1045 Vallejo Street, and at 40–42 Florence. He designed townhouses at 1, 3, 5, and 7 Russian Hill Place in 1915, shortly after the rich started moving onto the hill for its superb views. These and a few other buildings escaped the 1906 fire, but except for one block of Green Street, all of Russian Hill burned.

The 1000 block of Green, between Leavenworth and Jones, perfectly illustrates the schizophrenia Russian Hill succumbed to during the 1920s high-rise fever. At both ends of the historic block of old

Lombard Street residents have tried to get traffic barred here, but so far the city has decided that it's our inalienable right to drive down the wiggly block on Russian Hill.

dwellings, many-storied apartment buildings rise up and are visible from below. When the second stage of high-rises swept over Nob and Russian Hills in the 1960s, Russian Hill residents fought for a forty-foot

"If it pleases Providence to make a car run up and down a slit in the
ground for many miles and if for two pence half penny I can ride in that
car, why shall I ask the reason for the miracle."—Rudyard Kipling, 1891

building-height limit, which was enacted in 1974.

The architecture of the neighborhood now mixes post-earthquake Edwardian flat and brown-shingle houses with art deco and modern high-rises, small streets of pueblo-style stuccos (Florence Place), modern houses (65–66 Montclair Terrace), and large mansions (Francisco and Hyde). The Hyde/Powell cable car line clangs by a lot of these buildings, but you must explore on foot to find Macondray Lane, two blocks north of Coolbrith Park on Taylor. This landscaped pedestrian lane, so close to the city's downtown, is rural enough to hold a couple of old, funky, yellow clapboard houses in an overgrown garden.

Wander north from the end of Macondray Lane on Leavenworth to Francisco, where Jurgensen delivery boys bring delicacies to enormous, perfectly groomed mansions with mint-condition Mercedes cars in their huge garages. Right around the corner, at 800 Chestnut, a stream of punked-out art students pass in and out of the Spanish-revival-style San Francisco Art Institute. Perhaps the iconoclasm of Russian Hill's 1890s bohemia is reincarnated in the New Wave of the 1980s here.

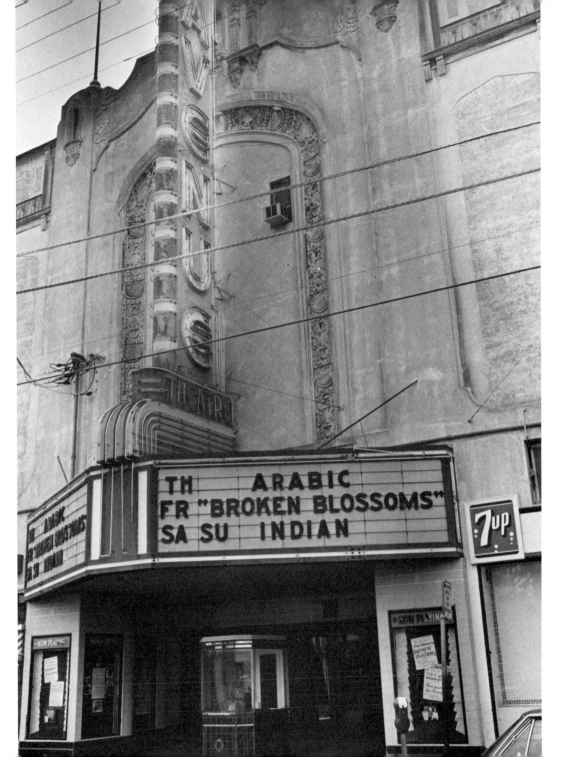

4

CIVIC CENTER · THE TENDERLOIN

Bums and winos snooze and shuffle through the finest group of Beaux Arts buildings in America. Well-to-do tourists hurrying from their hotels to the theater district carefully avoid the neighborhood street people hanging out around the corner of Mason and Turk Streets, the so-called "Transvestite Center." The trees on San Francisco's main commercial thoroughfare, Market Street, die from an excess of human urine.

The Civic Center and the Tenderloin, two downtown neighborhoods side by side on Market, probably have the worst reputations in San Francisco. Together with the nearby Western Addition, they account for almost all the rapes, murders, and robberies that take place in the city. Mayor Dianne Feinstein (who happens to own a residential hotel in the Tenderloin) has targeted the area as a number one priority for a clean up.

The Civic Center already shows evidence of this clean up. Inexpensive housing and a community center were demolished to make way for the Louise M. Davies Symphony Hall at Van Ness and Grove. More housing came down for the condominium complex known as "Opera Plaza." Newly renovated buildings house bright, stylish restaurants, such as Ivy's (398 Hayes) and the excellent Hayes Street Grill (324 Hayes). The prestigious Vorpal Gallery occupies a particularly attractive studio at 393 Grove.

Dick Callahan, a long-time resident of the area ("I didn't plan to stay for twenty-one years; it just evolved") has noticed the change. "It's definitely getting better, but rents get higher and housing tighter. There's a lot of office conversions now." He's not sorry to see some of the old buildings torn down ("They're havens for hippies, always on fire") and the area spruced up. But he could eventually be priced out

Tenderloin movie palaces declined with the advent of television. Many now cater to recent immigrants.

of the neighborhood he's lived in for more than two decades. "Sure, I've been mugged here, everyone has, but I like the neighborhood."

Perhaps the Civic Center is finally living up to its original promise as an example of Daniel Burnham's City Beautiful Movement. Burnham, a Chicago architect whose credo was, "Make no little plans; they have no magic to stir men's blood," was invited in 1905 to design a plan for San Francisco, which he did from his Twin Peaks cottage overlooking the city. Only the portions applying to the Civic Center and the Presidio Parkway materialized, however.

After the earthquake of 1906 caused the monstrously ugly City Hall to collapse in a matter of minutes, the city had the chance to implement Burnham's Civic Center plan. In 1911, the team of Bakewell and Brown came up with the winning design for the City Hall competition. Six more buildings—the Civic Auditorium, the public library, the federal office building, the state office building, the War Memorial Opera House, and Veterans' Auditorium—followed through 1936, creating a unified square of Beaux Arts architecture.

The latest addition to the block, Symphony Hall, unfortunately does not cut as elegant a figure as its neighbors, or even its earlier predecessor on the same site, Hayes Park. In the 1850s, Colonel Tom Hayes, for whom nearby Hayes Valley is named, erected on this site his estate, gardens and a three-story pavilion complete with concert hall, art gallery, and billiard parlor. The public flocked to the park's attractions until it burned down in 1872.

The Civic Center still attracts San Franciscans looking for entertainment and art. A fall arts festival is held around the reflecting pool, which is also the terminus for the Gay Freedom Day Parade held every June. Besides the San Francisco Symphony at Davies Hall, culture vultures patronize the San Francisco Opera and San Francisco Ballet, both at the Opera House, and the San Francisco Museum of Modern Art in Veterans' Auditorium. Chamber music, recitals, and small dance concerts are frequently held at the beautifully restored Herbst Theater (take particular note of the art nouveau murals), also in the Veterans' Auditorium.

Another type of museum, the African American Historical and Cultural Society's Sanderson Museum (680 McAllister), shows the art and history of black peoples around the world. Together with the predominantly black public housing nearby, it demonstrates that today's City Beautiful plan must include all races and classes.

While the Civic Center slowly yields to art and culture, fancy restaurants, and slick condos, its shabby neighbor, the Tenderloin, refuses to shape up into an "upgraded neighborhood." When I first saw the area, with its prostitutes and neon leg signs advertising "totally nude girls at the Paree," I thought "Tenderloin" referred to a human meat market. But according to Max Kirkeberg in *The District Handbook*, the name comes from the jargon of New York cops. In the nineteenth century, New York's finest received more for working a crime-infested beat than a tame one; thus, the rough-area assignment allowed policemen to buy the expensive tenderloin cut of beef.

The Tenderloin had always been a wild and lively place, until the 1906 earthquake leveled its vice parlors. The neighborhood was rebuilt with snazzy apartments and women's hotels, but soon the area fell back to its old tricks, and bordellos appeared, along with art deco movie palaces.

Hip new restaurants in renovated warehouses keep popping up in the
Civic Center. Recently completed Davies Symphony Hall, visible through
the window, is one reason for the revitalization of the neighborhood.

Apparently, the flicks contributed more to the Tenderloin's economy than the skin, because after television dealt the movie houses their death blow, the neighborhood reeled and collapsed. It became a center for recent immigrants, old people on fixed incomes, and, after 1960, an accepting haven for blacks and gays, who moved into its small apartments and residential hotels.

More old people live in the Tenderloin than anywhere else in the city—
most of them in relatively cheap residential hotels like this one.

Some gay professionals still live in the Tenderloin, but most of the area's residents are poor, old (more seniors live here than anywhere else in the city), black, Indochinese, or handicapped. The Tenderloin is a main reentry point for ex-convicts, as well as a hangout for runaway teenagers (at Mason and Eddy). But the statistics do not explain why many residents are willing to fight the city to keep their neighborhood the way it is.

According to the Planning Department, from 1975 to 1979 more than 6,000 residential hotel units were eliminated, mostly through conversion to tourist hotels. Since more than a third of the hotel residents are elderly or handicapped, which means that moving involves great difficulties for them, residents began to organize to fight evictions as well as the increase in tourism from the luxury hotels. Residents managed to achieve a moratorium on residential-hotel conversions and major concessions from Ramada and Holiday Inns for loans and funds for resident housing.

Ron Silliman, editor of the *Tenderloin Times*, told me that "encroachment into the area by hotels" has politicized residents such as those at the Dalt Hotel, who refused to move out for a conversion. "They feel noticed in the neighborhood. A maitre d' at Original Joe's [a good old San Francisco restaurant at 144 Taylor] used to walk one old lady back to the hotel every day. The people have support systems here." The Dalt is now one of four hotels the city has proposed to buy and make into low-cost housing.

Other hotels have worked out ratios. The Arlington, for instance, keeps its clientele at one-half tourist, one-quarter seniors, and one-quarter Arab Merchant Marine (there are all kinds of people here!). The Cadillac Hotel's ratio is about three-quarters seniors and one-quarter ex-cons. Owned by Reality House West, an organization for ex-offenders and ex-addicts, the hotel has a restaurant and a gym and is working well.

Other support systems Tenderloiners turn to are the Hospitality House, a warm and friendly center where classes and group meetings are held, and Glide Church, a Methodist congregation founded in 1929 at Ellis and Taylor. Glide's flamboyant minister, the Reverend Cecil Williams, is an outspoken defender of the down and out. Two communiques from the Symbionese Liberation Army (the radical group that kidnapped Patty Hearst) were addressed to Williams. His church encourages street people to attend the weekly "celebrations" of music, dance, and a rousing sermon by Williams. Taj Mahal and John Handy are just two of the many musicians who show up to play at Glide's Christmas and Easter services, which are followed by free meals and the distribution of free groceries.

Will the city allow the disenfranchised Tenderloiners to remain in their neighborhood, or will it replace the poor with free-spending tourists—and the old Edwardian buildings with modern high-rise hotels? Tenderloin residents are hoping that a humanistic approach will win out over economics. A shopping bag lady on Market summed it up this way: "We got a right to be alive somewheres, don't we?"

A superb collection of Victorians surrounds Alta Plaza in Pacific Heights.

5

WESTERN ADDITION

WRITER CHARLES CALDWELL DOBIE claimed that residents "love it for its supreme grotesqueness," but do residents of the Western Addition really love the neighborhood at all? When I asked Benny Stewart of the Western Addition Project Area Committee (WAPAC) about the advantages of living in the area, he answered, "There aren't many advantages in the Western Addition." Another resident, quoted in Jay Hansen's book, *The Other Guide to San Francisco*, explained why so many blacks from the area followed People's Temple leader Jim Jones to Guyana in 1977: "Just look around. There sure wasn't anything keeping them here."

While it is true that the Western Addition–Fillmore area is marked by deteriorating Victorians, run-down public housing, and empty lots, the neighborhood shows definite signs of revitalization. Many of those empty lots sprout vegetables carefully tended by local residents. Renovation of Victorian houses goes on here as well as in other parts of the city. And, since 1967, local activists in WAPAC have participated in the redevelopment of their neighborhood. The city's Redevelopment Agency relies on WAPAC so heavily that the RDA pays them over $100,000 in yearly contracts.

Good relations between the mostly black Western Addition residents and the RDA are relatively recent, however. In the early 1960s, Fillmore Street hopped to the beat of jazz and blues played at such clubs as Bop City and the Texas Playhouse, and shops lined the street. But the city saw this neighborhood of run-down Victorians as ideal for urban renewal. Mary Rogers, president of WAPAC, told the *San Francisco Neighborhood Perspective*, "It seems like a decision was made years ago to destroy the community. We had good buildings, old Victorians. They could have been rehabilitated. We tried to get the RDA not to tear the shops down, to get the owners to fix them up." But down they came, forcing many blacks to move out to the Bay View–Hunters Point area. The A-1 and A-2 urban renewal sites "swept the heart of the area clean, replacing black slum with upper middle-class high-rise," as *A Guide to Architecture in San Francisco and Northern California* duly noted.

Of course, urban renewal never helped the high crime, high unemployment, and poverty of the neighborhood; it just made the area uglier. But residents are determined to find minority contractors to build the proposed Fillmore Center, and to fill the center with shops and entertainment that serve the local community. As Mary Rogers said in the *San Francisco Examiner*, "I still won't let white folks take over this community. We will share it."

The history of the Western Addition is the history of the successive waves of ethnic groups coming to San Francisco. The city added the Western Addition onto its west boundary in 1851, but development started a full twenty years later, after Van Ness became a fashionable avenue. Middle-class rowhouses and nouveau riche Victorians dotted Pacific, California, and Fillmore Streets. Good examples of this era are found on Cottage Row, a charming little alley near Bush and Fillmore, and at 1801-45 Laguna.

Five eucalyptus trees at Bush and Octavia are the only reminder of one such Victorian, owned by Thomas Bell. The trees shade the smallest park in town, dedicated not to Bell, but to his mysterious black housekeeper, Mary Ellen (Mammy) Pleasant. Although her legend is shrouded in mystery, Mammy was believed to have been a former madam and cook who gave money to fleeing black slaves as well as to John Brown. Many San Franciscans speculated that Mammy pushed Thomas Bell to his death off the third-floor balcony. When Mammy died a few years later, her tombstone read, "Friend of John Brown."

By the turn of the century, families like the Bells had moved north to Pacific Heights or out of town, and the long process of ghettoizing the neighborhood had begun. After the 1906 earthquake destroyed their south-of-Market homes, many Jews moved into the undamaged Fillmore area. The southern end of Fillmore Street offered Jewish deli food and goods. The street experienced a boom after the devastation of Market Street in the earthquake. Merchants erected ornate wrought-iron arches of electric lights over the street to reflect their new prosperity (Director Erich von Stroheim filmed his classic silent film *Greed* on Fillmore in 1927). At the same time, Japanese established a neighborhood, Little Osaka, between Post and Sutter, and blacks moved in around Ellis and Scott.

But the area never did take off as residents had hoped. By World War II, the proud iron arches were taken down for scrap metal, the Japanese were forced out of their homes and interred in detention camps, and the Jews had moved out of the neighborhood. The war workers, particularly blacks, who had flocked to the city moved into the empty Victorian gingerbreads and Carpenter gothics.

Japanese returning to San Francisco after the war spread out over the city when they found their old homes occupied, but four percent of the Western Addition is still Japanese. The Japanese, like the blacks, also suffered through a redevelopment

Although Fillmore Street is a stark thoroughfare of discount stores and
empty lots right now, Western Addition residents plan to revitalize the
area with the shops and entertainment proposed in the Fillmore Center.

project—the Japan Center. Japanese Americans complain that to make room for this three-square-block, concrete structure (at Geary and Webster), which serves as a center for Japanese business interests and tourists, their houses were knocked down. A worker at the Committee against Nihonmachi Eviction told me that not only has the center dispersed the community, but it offers no services to old people and increases housing costs and gentrification (a term for areas reclaimed by the affluent who displace poor residents) problems. She stressed that because Japanese people come to the traditional Post/Buchanan area for a sense of identity, "It's important to maintain the area as a Japanese center."

While Japantown does not shelter the greatest proportion of Japanese Americans in the city (the Richmond has that distinction), it is very much a Japanese center. Japanese-language films show at the Kokusai Theater (1700 Post). Japanese- (and English-) language books are available at the wonderful Kinokuniya Bookstore, a great place to find lovely Japanese calendars with traditional woodcut illustrations. The bookstore, as well as a Japanese piano bar, Shinjuku, is located in the West Building of the Japan Center. Men can experience invigorating Shiatsu massage and relaxing hot baths at Kabuki Hot Spring. Dollmaking and flower arranging are both taught in the Japan Center, scene of numerous Japanese festivals during the year. Although there are at least fifteen Japanese restaurants in the Japan Center, the older restaurants outside the center, such as Osome (1945 Fillmore), seem folksier and more authentic.

Continuing down Fillmore, the passerby journeys through pockets settled by Eastern Europeans, Russians (the Museum of Russian Culture, a few blocks off Fillmore at 2450 Sutter, is open Saturdays 11 A.M.–3 P.M.), Filipinos, Scandinavians, Indians, and even Pathans, down around Fulton Street. This area between Alamo and Duboce parks is known as Hayes Valley, named in honor of the 160 acres here that Colonel Tom Hayes owned in the 1850s.

A decade later, San Franciscans took a steam train to The Chutes, an amusement park in what is now Buena Vista, but still they didn't develop the neighborhood until the 1870s; progress and deterioration followed in much the same fashion as in the upper Western Addition. Like the Western Addition, most of Hayes Valley is black, democratic, pro-labor, and poor. But gentrification looms larger here than in the area where A-1 redevelopment demolished a large part of the Victorian character.

Gays are moving north across Market Street to buy and renovate Victorians along Page Street between Pierce and Laguna. No one denies that spiffy Victorians improve the appearance of a neighborhood, but at the same time, rising rents push the poorer residents out of the area. Alamo Square, for years a crime-ridden, dirty park, displays some of the proudest Victorians in the city, such as the old Imperial Russian consulate at 1198 Fulton and the exquisite Victorian row along Steiner. Nearby, at 628 Divisadero, neighbors can listen to the high-quality jazz of Coke Escovedo and Babatunde at the V.I.S., a new club that is continuing the tradition of jazz in the Western Addition.

The crime, misconceived renewal projects, and poverty can't keep this neighborhood down. Local children flock to the banner-decorated Western Addition Cultural Center (762 Fulton) for classes in art, dance, and theater. The Buriel Clay Theater, also in the WACC, produces works by black playwrights, as does the Black Box Theater. Books on black life are stocked at New Day Bookstore (631 Divisadero), while many Asians patronize the bookstore at the Buddhist Churches of America at 1710 Octavia.

Whether they live in a condominium on Cathedral Hill, public housing at Marcus Garvey or Malcolm X Squares, or in a Victorian on Beidemann Place, the mixed population of the Western Addition is trying to make the neighborhood a place where there *are* advantages.

The Palace of Fine Arts, built as an eccentric ruins for the Panama-Pacific
Exhibition of 1915, now surrounds a lovely lagoon in the Marina and houses
a theater and a hands-on science museum, the Exploratorium.

6

PACIFIC HEIGHTS · MARINA COW HOLLOW

S AN FRANCISCANS GO ABSOLUTELY berserk over hills and views. They also go broke for them. A very general rule of thumb: the prettier the hill or the more spectacular the view, the higher the rent. Telegraph, Russian, and Nob Hills, Ashbury Heights and Seacliff, all cost you plenty to put out a mailbox, but the most exclusive of them all is Pacific Heights.

Together with the neighboring Marina, Cow Hollow, Presidio Heights, and Jordan Park, the area officially designated Supervisorial District Two holds more college graduates, more professionals and managers, and more families earning more than $25,000 a year than any other city district. Fewer minorities, Democrats, and liberal voters live here than elsewhere in the city. And it has been that way from the time the district grew up out of sand dunes, marshes, and willow forests in the last century.

The logical development of Presidio and Pacific Heights should have proceeded east from the Presidio after Juan Bautista de Anza claimed it in 1776. But the Spaniards preferred to lay a plank road on the steep ridge that runs along what are now Broadway and Divisadero to settle in the Mission District.

In 1836, Apolonario Miranda and his wife chose to settle not on the scenic ridge, but just below it, near a lagoon by the bay. Another Spaniard, Benito Diaz, sold this land for $1,000 to Thomas Larkin, almost as soon as Diaz himself got it. The Laguna Pequeña, or Washerwoman's Lagoon, drew settlers who appreciated clean clothes and fresh water for farming. William Hatman started a major trend in 1861 with his dairy farm, and soon the community changed its name from Spring Valley (one of the original springs still bubbles away in the courtyard of St. Mary's Episcopal Church at 2301 Union) to Cow Hollow, even though other businesses—a brewery, a tannery, and a bottler—shared the lagoon.

Cow Hollow boomed. Carriages and steam trains drew picnickers to Rudolf Herman's Harbor

View Park (now Yacht Harbor). Prominent citizens such as Frank Pixley, editor of the *Argonaut*, and William McElray moved to Cow Hollow (McElray's 1861 Octagon House at 2645 Gough is still standing and open to the public on the second and fourth Thursday afternoon of each month). Even the pollution of the lagoon by open sewage, cows, and industry failed to slow down the growth of Cow Hollow. The city simply ordered the cows out of the area forever in 1891 and put prisoners to work filling in the putrid lagoon with sand from the dunes at Lombard Street.

While Cow Hollow moved into its second phase of shopkeeping and industry in the 1890s, San Francisco's upper crust discovered Pacific Heights. The duck and dairy farms, such as the one owned by Captain Charles Gulliver in the 1860s, shared Pacific Heights with a few small Victorians in the 1870s. Jeweler J. W. Tucker built a modest Victorian housing development for working-class people between Jackson, Washington, Webster, and Buchanan Streets about the time that a cable car line came through in 1878.

Just as the cable car induced the rich to leave Rincon Hill for Nob Hill, now it lured many of them to huge Victorians in Pacific Heights. A few managed the address without benefit of the deed. Samuel W. Holladay, a wily attorney, claimed Lafayette Square, which had been declared a park in 1867, by squatting on it. No traditional squatter tents for him, though. He built a mansion, a barn, a windmill, and the state's second observatory, while successfully fighting off the city right past his death in 1915 at age 91. The city finally reclaimed the park in 1935 but had to pay $200,000 to get it.

Van Ness Avenue, five feet wider than Market Street, became the Champs Elysees of San Francisco, with plush mansions, lush landscaping, and convenient cable cars. The 1906 earthquake squashed the street's pretensions, however, when the fire department declared it a firebreak and dynamited the street. Van Ness rapidly decayed into a noisy thoroughfare and automobile-showcase row that killed the last cable car line in 1956.

Eastern Pacific Heights, like Russian and Nob Hills, sprouted luxury apartment houses, but unlike the older hills, the buildings rarely grew more than eight stories high. A few of the original Victorians remain in the area. The 1886 Haas-Lilienthal House (2007 Franklin), restored by the Foundation for Architectural Heritage, is open to the public on Wednesday and Sunday afternoons. Its grey hue was a standard house color in Victorian days.

The red sandstone Whittier Mansion, built in 1896 at 2090 Jackson for a paint store king, now houses the California Historical Society and is open to the public Wednesday, Saturday, and Sunday afternoons. Germany owned the building for two months in 1941, until the United States declared war and seized it.

After the earthquake and fire, San Francisco determined to show the world "the city that refused to die," arising from the ashes like the phoenix of the city's seal in one of the grandest, most opulent fairs of all time—the Panama-Pacific Exhibition of 1915. Although the fair ostensibly celebrated the opening of the Panama Canal, it really served as San Francisco's open house, drawing more than 18 million visitors. The city filled in about 600 acres of a large marsh area right on the bay north of Cow

Paintings compete with the view of Gas House Cove outside the
windows of a gallery in Fort Mason. The old army buildings now house
theaters, music clubs, dance studios, and a restaurant.

Hollow and east of the Presidio. There were built, besides the Zone amusement park, such art nouveau spectacles as the Tower of Jewels and ten exhibit halls. One San Franciscan recalled that she never saw anything so beautiful as the exhibition at night. "I thought I might as well die the night they closed it down, because I'd never see anything so wonderful again. Everyone was crying."

A new neighborhood, the Marina, took the place of the exhibit. How appropriate that the Marina Civic Improvement Association, with the subsequent financial help of Walter Johnson, saved one of the exhibition's temporary buildings, Bernard Maybeck's Palace of Fine Arts. The palace still stands by a pond in a green park at Bay and Lyon, and holds a theater and a science museum, the Exploratorium.

The Marina reflects the Mediterranean and Spanish revival architecture popular in the 1920s. Most of the low, single-family buildings sport a garage, an indication of the growing desire for automobiles. The streets break from the typical grid of the city into a curvy pattern, but they can't help the basic dullness of the undistinguished pastel houses.

Marina residents remain fiercely loyal to their very stable, upper-middle-class, white neighborhood. Linda Jue, a young native San Franciscan who lives in the Marina, explains, "There's shopping on Chestnut or Union, the Palace of Fine Arts, bike-riding in the Presidio, kite-flying on Marina Green, the bay, easy access to Marin, and lot's happening at Fort Mason."

Another resident, an Italian American woman who's lived in the Marina for fifty years, likes the stability. "It started out about 75 percent Italian, and I think it's still Italian. Young people grow up,

Trendy young professionals patronize the boutiques, bars, and restaurants housed in restored Victorians along Union Street in Cow Hollow.

marry and have families here [actually only 13 percent of the Marina's population of around 20,000 is under 17 years old]. It just shows that this is not a transient city. Everybody who criticizes it doesn't know anything, including the supervisors." She's worried about the Presidio—"We need the jobs and want the army to stay"—and about Fort Mason—"We're not pleased with Fort Mason at all. Cultural my foot. We wanted a park, not a Chinese Trade Show or the other stuff they sell there."

The older residents might be leery of Fort Mason, but others like what's happened to the old army post at Laguna and Marina. The former barracks now house the innovative Magic Theater, the Oceanic Society, four art galleries, Plowshares Coffee House, the beautiful vegetarian restaurant, Greens, as well as dozens of classes and workshops.

Marina residents fear attractions that would start a crowded boutique trend similar to that which is all too visible on Cow Hollow's Union Street. Cow Hollow always supported a commercial area on Union, but in the 1950s, the antique and gift stores began to supplant the cleaners, five-and-dimes, and grocers. Entrepreneurs appreciated the fine collection of Victorians available on the street. Old landmarks, such as the twin wedding houses at 1980 Union (so called because they were a father's identical wedding gifts to his two daughters), became refurbished restaurants and boutiques. The three hundred or so fashionable shops, bars, and restaurants on Union Street today attract enough tourists to congest the area, a problem Marina residents prefer to avoid by frequenting their own commercial street, Chestnut.

Most traffic passes through the Marina on Lombard Street, which is also Route 101. But a growing number of San Franciscans now detour through Chestnut for the fine Japanese food at Kichihei (2084 Chestnut), elegant Italian cuisine at

The view-blocking apartment houses built in the 1960s spurred Russian Hill residents to push for a forty-foot building-height limit, which they got in 1974.

La Pergola (2060 Chestnut), or live bluegrass music at Paul's Saloon (3251 Scott).

The entry by the western Pacific Heights-Presidio Heights (the area adjacent to the Presidio)

Sugar King Adolph Spreckels's ostentatious French Baroque mansion fits
right in with the other mansions near Lafayette Park. Spreckels also
built the Palace of the Legion of Honor, in Lincoln Park.

area into the contest for the "cutesiest" shopping area is Sacramento Street. Right now the street still mixes auto repair garages and an old movie theater with high-priced gift shops and such classy restaurants as the Tuba Garden (3634 Sacramento), well-known for its lovely outdoor courtyard.

Many tourists visiting Pacific Heights skip the shopping in favor of the architecture. While some of the large mansions have only their size to commend them, many others are the work of San Francisco's best architects, including Bernard Maybeck, Willis Polk, Ernest Coxhead, and William Knowles. All these luminaries worked on a superb block of shingled houses lined up on the steep 3200 block of Pacific Avenue in the early 1900s. Works by a younger generation of architects can also be found in the area. William Wurster (250 and 301 Locust, 2560 Divisadero), Joseph Esherick (3700 Washington, 3323 Pacific), and H. T. Howard (2944 Jackson) are among the most prominent architects here.

One of the oldest houses in the area, the Italianate Casebolt House (2727 Pierce), dates back to 1865. Rowhouses of a slightly later period line up on the 2600 block of Clay Street on the southern border of Alta Plaza Park. This group may be San Francisco's most photographed cluster of Victorians. The southern side of Lafayette Park, at 2080 Washington, showcases the Adolph Spreckels mansion, a French baroque palace built in 1913 for the son of a sugar king. Later, in 1924, the architect, George Applegarth, and Spreckels built the California Palace of the Legion of Honor in Lincoln Park, a special interest of Spreckels' French wife Alma de Bretteville.

Private ownership of such enormous buildings couldn't last. Many of the old mansions now house schools or religious orders. A surprising 80 percent of Pacific Heights residents rent, rather than own, their homes. But the privileged society there still crowds opera galas, symphony openings, and ballet fundraisers, and read about themselves in Pat Montandon's society column in the San Francisco Examiner. The debutante and her cavalier are alive and well on Pacific Heights.

The expensive Mediterranean-style houses in Sea Cliff command
striking views of the Bay and Golden Gate Bridge.

7

THE RICHMOND

SHORTLY AFTER NEWSPAPERMAN Sam Brannan opened the Cliff House Resort at Land's End in 1863, another newpaperman, Samuel Clemens, a.k.a. Mark Twain, undertook what he thought would be a pleasant outing to the new resort and beach. However, the trip turned out to be a "six-mile ride in the clouds; but if I ever have to take another, I want to leave the horse in the stable and go in a balloon. There was not much dust, because the gale blew it all to Oregon in two minutes" (from *The Golden Era*). Twain had just experienced his first summer in the Richmond District, or the "Great Sand Waste," as early maps described it. No one knows if it was that particular beach trip that prompted Twain's assertion that "the coldest winter I ever spent was summer in San Francisco."

San Francisco annexed the windy, foggy northwest section of flat dune lands under the Consolidation Act of 1856, but more than fifty years passed before inner-city crowding induced residents to move out onto them, dubbed the Richmond. Prior to 1900, most of the San Franciscans residing in the Richmond were dead—peaceful inhabitants of either the Municipal Golden Gate Cemetery, at Clement and 33rd Avenue, or the Chinese Cemetery, at Land's End (although both cemeteries were moved at the turn of the century, stone entrances to an old Chinese tomb still stand in Lincoln Park's golf course).

After a toll road cut through the Richmond in 1863, a few people began operating roadhouses in the district. A few more moved to the area after a racetrack opened and title claims were settled in 1866. At about this time, the city laid out a grid pattern for the area, put aside 1,000 acres for Golden Gate Park, and planned to flatten the sand dunes. But Adolph Sutro, an engineer who made a fortune in the Comstock Lode, accelerated the development of the area in the 1880s, for which he deserves the title "Father of the Richmond."

First Sutro gave the people an incentive to visit

the area. He bought and remodeled the burned Cliff House, erected the fabulous glass-enclosed Sutro Baths (a group of public swimming pools right on the ocean), and built his own house and elaborate gardens (open free to the public) above the Cliff House, where Sutro Park is today. His only neighbors at the time were the rag-tag followers of Con Mooney and Denis Kearney, the anti-Chinese labor leader, who lived in Mooneysville below the Cliff House on Ocean Beach.

After supplying San Franciscans with a reason to brave the fog and wind, Sutro provided the means to do it. He built a steam railroad on California Street and charged the public a nickel a ride. After selling this first line to Southern Pacific, he started an electric trolley line on Clement Street to compete with it, still charging 5¢.

Sadly enough, Sutro's attractions are now just ghosts of their former selves. Buses have replaced his steam railroad, and only an ugly box stands on the site of his Victorian-fantasy Cliff House, razed by fire in 1907. A few marble statues, a foundation, and a kiosk are all that remain of the Sutro mansion. A ruin of caves, steps, and broken pools commemorates the once-spectacular baths, destroyed by fire in 1969. Nevertheless, all Sutro's projects did succeed in their original purpose—to attract potential residents to the Richmond.

Thousands of single-family, middle-class houses popped up between 1910 and 1930, stimulated by an electric Muni line built on Geary in 1912. A few low-rise apartment buildings appeared on the main east-west drags of Geary, Clement, and California Streets. Unlike the Sunset District, which was developed later, the Avenues of the Richmond sprouted houses one by one rather than in identical blocks, so the Richmond retained a small-town atmosphere.

A few wealthy sections developed in the area. Presidio Terrace, a small circle below the Presidio, featured single-family houses when built in 1905, but the Great Depression turned it into subdivided, middle-class flats. In 1912, Mark Daniels began an exclusive development of about seventy-five houses on the cliffs between Lincoln Park and the Presidio, right near Phelan Beach, a former Chinese fishing camp. The large, pastel, Mediterranean-style houses, which take in the view along the curvy streets, are attractive if not architecturally notable. Willis Polk designed the houses at 9, 25, and 45 Scenic Way. A more modern house by Wurster, Bernardi, and Emmons (850 El Camino) sits across the street from another recent residence by Joseph Esherick (895 El Camino).

On November 19, 1917, the Richmond District was officially renamed Park Presidio by city ordinance. Perhaps a proud new Richmondite disliked the old associations of sand, waste, and fog that clung to the old name. However, the new name obviously never stuck.

After World War I, Russians and Eastern European Jews moved into the district; their religious centers are still major landmarks at either end of the Richmond. Temple Emanu-El, in the Inner Richmond (Arguello at Lake), draws its congregation from the largest concentration of Jews in the city (although most of the Jews of San Francisco are scattered throughout most areas). The gold-domed Cathedral of the Holy Virgin (Geary at 26th Avenue) is the place to go for Pasxa, the Russian Orthodox Easter. Each year, the police cordon off two lanes of

Richmond kids soon learn that one plays in the sun at Baker Beach only
in spring or fall. The beach is socked in by fog most of the summer.

Geary Boulevard to accommodate the crowds of Russians and curious bystanders who gather on the night before Easter to watch elaborately costumed priests and choir parade around the church three times in search of Christ's body. At midnight, bulbs light up outside the church and everyone calls out *"Xristos Voskrese"* (Christ is risen) and exchange kisses and candles. The mass ends at around 3 A.M.

Card players while away a sunny afternoon at Mountain Lake Park,
while more active park visitors jog around the nearby lake.

Russian restaurants and businesses still thrive in the Richmond. The Miniature Bakery (433 Clement), Cinderella Bakery (436 Balboa), Acropolis Delicatessen (5217 Geary), Renaissance Restaurant (5241 Geary), and Znanie Russian Bookstore (5237 Geary) are just a few of the Russian establishments in the Richmond.

A second wave of ethnic groups piled into the Richmond after World War II, mostly from other San Francisco neighborhoods. More Jews came to the Richmond from their old Fillmore neighborhood, where black wartime workers now lived. The Japanese, returning from the concentration camps in the desert, found their Western Addition homes occupied, and many moved on to the Richmond. Today, despite the Japan Center Complex in the Western Addition, more Japanese Americans live in the Richmond than in any other neighborhood in the city. They make up 6 percent of the neighborhood population and live mostly in the outer Richmond.

The Irish moved west across the city after the war. The Blarney Stone (Geary at 21st Avenue) and the Plough and Stars (116 Clement) are only two of the many Irish bars that line the main thoroughfares. There's even an Irish bookstore, Alicorn (3428 Balboa).

Many Chinese wanted to buy homes outside of Chinatown, but racist laws excluded them from that privilege until the late 1940s. In the 1950s, so many Chinese bought houses along Clement Street between 1st and 11th Avenues that some people call this area "New Chinatown." The Chinese are the largest minority group in the Richmond. They make up 15 percent of the population there, which accounts for the profusion of Chinese restaurants. Members of the Chinese and Japanese community established the Asian American Theater Company at 4344 California, a nationally known group that produces new plays by Asians under the guidance of playwright Frank Chin.

Clement Street in particular reflects the ethnic diversity of the area. Besides Irish bars, Chinese restaurants, and Russian bakeries, you might find the all-American burger at Bill's Place (2315 Clement), comedy at the Holy City Zoo (408 Clement), country music at the Last Day Saloon (406 Clement), and East Indian foods at Haig's Delicacies.

Out of a district population of around 62,000, 63 percent are white and 56 percent foreign-born, with very few blacks, Latinos, or Filipinos living in the Richmond, however. The neighborhood remains staunchly middle class and married. More than half the adults have high school diplomas and jobs as skilled laborers. Their life here is quiet, surrounded by Golden Gate Park to the south, Ocean Beach and Sutro Park to the west, and Lincoln Park and the Presidio to the north. The Richmond contains more residential land than any other city district, and that's how residents want it to stay.

This is a neighborhood where old men play card games all day long in a metal lean-to by a little-known lake where Juan Bautista de Anza camped with his soldiers in 1776 (Mountain Lake Park, 8th Avenue at Lake). It has beaches with seals, large, impressive houses on cul-de-sacs (West Clay Park), and endless streets of blank stucco rows. And, of course, the Richmond has one of the coldest, foggiest, windiest summers Mark Twain ever saw.

Vermont Street between 20th and 22nd is just as curvy as the more
famous Lombard Street, but without the crowds or flowers.

8

SOUTH OF MARKET
POTRERO HILL

SINCE HERB CAEN did such a complete job of killing the nickname "Frisco," maybe he should be enlisted to suppress the sobriquet SoMa, for South of Market. SoMa sounds too derivative of New York's SoHo, and while both areas are warehouse districts that attract artists, that's about the extent of their similarity.

San Francisco's South of Market seems to serve as a catch-all for any and everything that couldn't or wouldn't fit in elsewhere. Gay S&M bars, punk rock hangouts, a couple of bus terminals, artists and alternative galleries, a tattoo museum, old folks on fixed incomes, empty breweries, a wholesale flower market, the hole dug for the underground George Moscone Convention Center, and a park built especially for bums and winos—all of this is crammed into flatlands surrounded by freeways, the Embarcadero piers, and the Maginot Line of Market Street.

Except for the once-grand homes of Rincon Hill and South Park, South of Market has always been the home turf of the poor, the recent immigrant, and industry. Soon after Jasper O'Farrell mapped the swamps and inlets of the area in 1847, a tent city of squatters grew up on the huge lots of the breweries, tanneries, refineries, and the like that characterized the area.

In the 1850s, J. C. Christian Russ, a landlord whose estate covered the 6th Street and Howard block, offered the use of his gardens to the wide variety of ethnic groups for their celebrations. A different group of people now party at just about the same spot. The down-and-out rejects of San Francisco gather at Street People's Park under the auspices of Cecil Williams' Glide Church. The park features extra-wide benches for napping, although the sleeping tubes were removed when territorial fights broke out over them. Such a park could exist only in San Francisco.

During the 1870s, the Irish lived around Howard Street, the Greeks occupied the degenerating Rincon

Hill, and the Japanese moved into shabby South Park. Jews lived on Tehama, Clara, Shipley, and Clementina Streets betwen Howard and Harrison, 5th and 6th Streets, but after the 1906 quake destroyed the South o' the Slot (so named for the cable car slot on Market Street), these small sidestreets buckled and sank on their quicksand bases. Jewish residents had no desire to live in the bizarrely tilting structures, so they moved to the Fillmore. Walk by 479 and 483 Tehama or 274 Shipley for some graphic earthquake reminders.

The immigrants who were burned out in 1906 never did return. Industry and a Skid Row quickly filled in the old residential areas. Even today, South of Market is almost half industry. A new wave of immigrants poured in after World War II, and now more Filipinos live here than anywhere else in the city. South of Market is about one-third Latino, more than a third white, and one-tenth black. One-fifth of the residents are over 60 years old and a third of the people earn less than $4,000 a year.

Just as gays moved into Polk Gulch and the Tenderloin during the 1960s for the live-and-let-live anonymity, so they gravitated toward South of Market, which offered the same ambience. Now gays contribute to the high number of singles here. Folsom Street is the heart of the hardcore gay nightlife, with such bars and businesses as The Stud (1535 Folsom) and The Trading Post (960 Folsom). Folsom Street also has a few very unique restaurants. Hamburger Mary's (1582 Folsom) is loud, cheap, and very odd. Augusta's South of Market Grill (1256 Folsom) is neither odd nor loud, but its outside eating area is an unusual feature in the heart of industry land. The Rite Spot Cafe (2099 Folsom) is up the street from the excellent Oberlin Dance Collective. The Rite Spot looks like your typical hole in the wall, but inside there's original art on the walls, white linen on the tables, and fine Continental food.

The Rite Spot caters to South of Market's newest residents, the artists, dancers, and musicians who like the low rents they pay for huge warehouse spaces. Resident artists in the formerly ugly Hamm's Brewery have knocked out walls and created a rainbow lighting effect. And alternative galleries have appeared in profusion: Jetwave (1151 Market), A.R.E. (1141 Market), S.O.M.A. Gallery (2795 16th Street), and Site (585 Mission). Performance art pieces, ranging from a dramatization of one man's thirty years in his Vallejo garage to exhibitions of video art, happen at La Mamelle (70 12th Street), 80 Langton Street, AAA Studios (233 14th Street), and South of Market Cultural Center (934 Brannan). The last time I went to the Hotel Utah (500 4th Street) for a comedy show, I had a drink with a heavily made-up three-foot-tall woman dressed in red velvet and feathers. Lyle Tuttle's Tattoo Art Museum is also South of Market—where else could it be?

All this action is starting to spill over into China Basin, right next door on the bay. In the 1870s, China Basin was Mission Bay, a waterway clogged with piers and boats (including Clippers headed for China, hence the name). Mission Bay, like many other San Francisco waterways, became landfilled, but shipping continued into the 1900s. Everyone knows that the Oakland Port surpassed San Francisco because Oakland built piers to handle container ships. But San Francisco does have one containerized pier at China Basin.

Before these sleeping tubes were moved from Street People's Park at
6th and Howard, bums and winos claimed them as home. The street people
still gather in this "only in San Francisco" park.

Waterfront buffs hang out at the old houseboats, the harbor, and the drawbridge at Mission Creek Marina. They eat at some of the wonderful al fresco bars and restaurants on the water here, untouched by conventioneer or tourist. The funky, sunny Mission Rock Resort (817 China Basin) is a favorite of all kinds of people, especially the fishermen who tie up right below the outside deck. The Wharfside (185 Berry Street) and the Sailing Ship (Pier 42) are also worth a visit.

China Basin shows signs of becoming an area of high-tech industrial parks, so the live-loose atmosphere of the basin may not survive too much longer. Artists are staking their claims in some of the dormant canning buildings, one of which houses the China Basin Dance Theater.

China Basin was once connected to Potrero Hill by a mile-long causeway across old Mission Bay. Now Mission Creek and the two freeways cut Potrero off from the basin, South of Market, and the Mission. Like its neighbors, much of Potrero Hill land is industrial. But unlike South of Market or China Basin, almost half of Potrero's residents live in single-family houses that many of them own.

These small Victorian or nondescript frame houses stretch up and down the steep slopes of Potrero Hill to take advantage of the superb views of downtown, the bay, or the Mission. On the balmy, fog-free summer evenings the Potrero is famous for, residents stroll the hill with children and dogs, pausing to chat with neighbors or to pick up a copy of the *Potrero View* newspaper.

The Potrero Neighborhood House (953 De Haro) is a major gathering place for the community, providing recreation and jobs for teenagers and seniors as well as a home for the Julian Theater,

noted for productions of German avant-garde plays. A worker at the Neighborhood House cited the "willingness to discuss problems openly, and pride in the neighborhood and its history" as identifying traits of the Potrero Hill dweller.

In recent years, many white professionals have "discovered" the advantages of life on Potrero Hill in such condominium projects as Victorian Mews. But the neighborhood remains (at least for the time being) working class and heterogeneous. Blacks and Latinos make up about half of the population, mostly around the Potrero Hill Recreation Center. A group of Russian Molokans have lived on the hill since they emigrated here after the Russo-Japanese War of 1905. The Russian Full Gospel Church (884 Rhode Island) and the First Russian Christian Church (841 Carolina) are Molokan centers. Aging hippies in handmade houses cluster around the 25th Street/De Haro section. Synanon takes up a block on 23rd Street at the bottom of the hill.

There's nothing left of the original Mission pasture for which the Spanish named Potrero Hill. When the Mexicans controlled California, they granted Potrero Hill to the sons of Francisco de Haro, the first *alcalde*, or mayor, of Yerba Buena. Soon after the Gold Rush, ranches shared Potrero Hill with a slaughterhouse, Union Iron Works, and a mining equipment company. For a time in the 1880s, the hill became known as Scotch Hill for all the Scots who moved in to work at Union Iron.

Irish ironworkers settled in Dogpatch (the eastern section of Potrero, once overrun with packs of

A typical Victorian cottage on Potrero Hill. Poet Lawrence Ferlinghetti once lived here.

dogs) at 20th Street and Illinois on Irish Hill, where they boarded in the Shasta House or Jim Gately's San Quentin and drank steam beer and boxed in Mike Boye's Saloon. All that's left of Irish Hill today is a small concrete-covered slope surrounded by steel-yards. After Bethlehem Steel took over Union Iron, the company cut the hill away to make room for the expanding plant.

Spanish-speaking workers of the Southern Pacific Railroad moved up the hill during the Depression, followed a decade later by black war workers. The artists, students, and gays who moved into South of Market and China Basin spread into Potrero in the 1970s.

The thriving community gardens at McKinley Square (Vermont and 20th Streets) are a result of this neighborhood's ability to absorb a variety of ethnic groups. As the neighbors work in the gardens, their children play in a park with one of the best views in San Francisco. A great Potrero pleasure is a breath-taking city panorama seen from the swings hanging out over the end of the park. Afterwards, drive down Vermont Street, between 20th and 22nd Streets, for a crooked road as curvy as Lombard but minus the crowds.

Potrero Hill is definitely not touristy. The stores along 20th Street and Missouri are utilitarian, not boutiquelike. Three modest restaurants are worth checking out, though. The W&J Cafe (849 22nd Street) offers good Southern-style food, and Klein's (501 Connecticut) is just the spot to pick up a Jewish deli picnic for a warm day in McKinley Square. S. Asimakopoulos (288 Connecticut) serves excellent, reasonably priced Greek specialties at tables deco-rated with vases of fresh orchids. Try finding that touch of class anywhere else but Potrero Hill.

9

DEATH OF AN OLD NEIGHBORHOOD

THE TYPICAL NEIGHBORHOOD in the typical American city changes class, race, and style every few generations, possibly becoming dormant for a while but rarely becoming extinct. San Franciscans like to think of their city as atypical, and they're right in the case of Rincon Hill/South Park, a once-fashionable neighborhood between Folsom, Brannan, Fremont, and 3rd Streets that died.

After the Gold Rush, San Francisco's rich and solid citizens built on Rincon, the sunny hill overlooking the bay, and on nearby South Park, an oval green reminiscent of London's Berkeley Square. A bishop, the photographer Eadweard Muybridge, and George Hearst all lived in fine mansions on Rincon Hill. Perhaps the hill was jinxed, because these three, as well as the hill itself, suffered catastrophes here. Muybridge discovered his wife's

infidelity and shot her lover. Hearst lost much of his Comstock Lode money and had to sell his brick house in 1874. (Hearst later recouped his fortune and bought the San Francisco *Examiner*, mostly to aid his political aspirations. Apparently owning the paper didn't help him enough. He lost his election bid for governor in 1882, but managed to get appointed to the U.S. Senate four years later. His son, William Randolph, took over the *Examiner* after being expelled from Harvard.) In the late 1860s, the bishop's house fell in when the city cut into the hill to grade new streets.

All this bad luck was too much for the resident nabobs, who soon moved up to Nob Hill and Pacific Heights. At the time of the quake, sailors' hotels and grimy flophouses dotted Rincon and South Park. Herb Caen described Rincon's final humiliation as

Old buildings tilting on Tehama Street bear witness to the
powerful shakes of the 1906 earthquake.

occurring in the 1930s when the hill "lost its chic and then its head under the Bay Bridge approaches," the warehouses, the Union Oil Tower, and the Transbay Bus Terminal.

Rincon's gone for good, but there is hope of a new eruption for South Park. The oval and a few shabby Victorians still stand between 2nd, 3rd, Brannan, and Bryant Streets, inhabited by the poor and a few artists. When the waterfront is redeveloped, South Park may either be bulldozed for good or designated a historic landmark.

After a visit to South Park, ponder the area's future over lunch at Ruby's (4th Street and Brannan), or Blanche's (998 4th Street). Both restaurants have attractive outside patios that prove you don't have to be rundown and ugly just because your neighbors are warehouses and traintracks.

Twenty-fourth and Mission, where most people-watching, parades,
fiestas, and action happen in the neighborhood.

10

THE MISSION
BERNAL HEIGHTS

THE LONG, DENSELY SETTLED Mission Valley, sheltered between Twin Peaks and Potrero Hill, could possibly be called a ghetto, since about half the residents here are Latino and poor. But no one ever refers to the area as a ghetto. The word conjures up the violent slums of the East Los Angeles *barrio*, or New York's Spanish Harlem, but certainly not San Francisco's thriving Mission District.

The Mexicans, Guatemalans, Nicaraguans, Salvadoreans, Colombians, and other South and Central Americans who make up the majority of the Mission's population have done more than bring back Spanish to the old Mission of Padre Palou. Wall paintings after the style of the great Mexican muralists adorn storefronts and Bart train plazas. Shoppers of all ages jam 24th Street to buy fresh fish, vegetables, and tortillas at the markets. Gringos walk the street for the inexpensive but often excellent Mexican restaurants and the films at the York

Theatre. Modern dancers studying at Dancentral or the Margaret Jenkins Studio jostle teenagers disco dancing on street corners to the sound of an oversized transistor radio.

When I was in high school, kids cruised the main streets of town looking for action. Cool kids of the Mission cruise in large, mint-condition American cars, sometimes outfitted with red plush carpeting or chandeliers, but always sporting a hydraulic system that pumps the car up and down. These low-riders listen to sixties 'soul and Motown while they drive *very* slowly up Mission Street. Lately these clubs of low-riders claim they've been harassed out of the Mission by the police, but they'll no doubt be back to ride in the Cinco de Mayo parade, celebrating Mexico's 4th of July.

The Mission is no perpetual fiesta, however. In 1979, the district police station reported the highest number of aggravated assaults in the city and the second highest number of rapes (after the Western Addition). Gays attracted to the restorable Victorians in the neighborhood have encountered hostility, macho taunts, and even bashings. Two men that teenagers perceived to be gay were severely beaten in Dolores Park in 1980.

A number of women's businesses and bars, such as Good Vibrations, Amelia's, and Old Wives Tales Books, exist quietly on Valencia Street most of the time, but last year the Women's Building on 18th Street near Valencia was damaged by a hidden bomb.

Many old people with tiny incomes live along Valencia Street, where they're often victimized by young hoods. The Mission has more children aged 5-17 years than any other district. Most residents are skilled laborers who earn $4,000-$10,000 a year, rent their homes, and struggle with the high unemployment and real estate speculation that plague the district.

The Mission Cultural Center tries to head off problems by sponsoring discussions about the issues. Both the center and *El Tecolote*, the ten-year-old Mission newspaper, provide a much needed forum for Latino residents.

It's almost poetic justice that Spanish is once again spoken up and down the Mission, because this is where the Spanish explorers and padres established their church and village in 1776. Captain Gaspar de Portola had discovered San Francisco Bay only six years before Captain Juan Bautista de Anza marked the lakeside site of the new Mission in 1775. Anza named the lake Laguna de Nuestra Senora de los Dolores (Our Lady of the Sorrows) on the Virgin's Day, the Friday before Palm Sunday. By 1791, Padre Francisco Palou had dedicated to St. Francis of Assisi the adobe church he had designed, but the lake's name, Dolores, became the popular name of the mission.

The warm, fog-free valley that attracted the Spaniards had earlier drawn the Ohlone Indians, who settled a small village they called Awaa-te. The Ohlone were a peaceable, generally nomadic tribe of the Costanoan, or Coast people, who lived on seafood fished from a lagoon off Mission Bay. Soon after the arrival of the Spanish, the Ohlone found themselves cut off from their old way of life and forced into the Mission village, where they were quickly wiped out by European diseases. In 1850, according to Randolph Delehanty in his book *San Francisco*, a United States Indian agent could find only one Indian survivor, Pedro Alcantara: "I am all that is left of my people—I am alone." More than 5,000 Indians are buried in the Mission Dolores's cemetery. Almost all that was left to commemorate the Costanoan culture was the beautiful mission ceiling painted with Costanoan basket designs.

The Mission District passed from Indian to Spanish and then Mexican hands. The huge Mexican land grants given to Juan Francisco Bernal, a soldier under Anza in 1776, and Jose de Jesus Noe, the last *alcalde* of San Francisco, when Mexico seceded from Spain in 1821 became a squatters' paradise in the next couple of decades. The Van Ness Ordinance of 1855 deemed squatters in the Mission and Western Addition bona fide landowners and citizens of San Francisco.

With the Americans, of course, came development: a forty-foot-wide plank toll road in 1851 (now Market Street), the first city railroad in 1857, and industry on Mission Creek. During the 1860s, San

Not everyone loves mariachi music. Maybe this guy would be
happier at one of the many jazz clubs in the Mission.

Franciscans poured into the Mission to see a Chinese giant, wild animals, exotic flora, and dazzling statuary at Woodward's Gardens (a plaque commemorates the attraction at Mission and Duboce Streets). From 1870 to 1900, the population in the Mission grew from 23,000 to 36,000.

Other than Mission Dolores, not a trace of the Spanish remained. The rowhouses built on speculation going up everywhere were Victorian, and many still exist, such as the row on Capp Street between 22nd and 23rd or the group at Guerrero and Duboce. The rich drove to the Mission on Sunday afternoons to promenade down the boulevard in their fine carriages. The *laguna* was filled in and the land around the church turned into two Jewish cemeteries, which later, in 1905, became Dolores Park. Baseball fans took in San Francisco Seals games at the park on Valencia and 15th Streets from 1907 until 1930, and after that at Seals Stadium at 16th and Bryant Streets (now deserted for foggy Candlestick Park).

Yankees, Germans, and Scandinavians settled into the Mission. After the fire of 1906 raged through North Beach and South of Market, bumbling dynamiters somehow managed to blow up Dolores Street as far as 17th Street, supposedly to save the mission. Still, much of the area escaped the flames unscathed and became a prime refugee center for homeless Italian and Irish San Franciscans. The new natives developed a "Mish" accent, which sounded a little like Brooklynese according to some old-timers.

As if anticipating the new wave of Hispanic peoples immigrating to the Mission, the residents began cultivating a Spanish revival in their neighborhood. Willis Polk restored and stuccoed the old Mission Dolores (it easily rode out the quake that destroyed the new church next door), a new basilica was built in a vaguely Spanish style, John McLaren (the Scottish landscaper of Golden Gate Park) planted palms along Dolores Street, and Mission High School sported a red tile roof.

But the Mission's charms as a solid, middle-class neighborhood waned after World War II. Everybody wanted to live in a suburb, such as the Excelsior or Crocker-Amazon areas south of Mission. The middle class that moved to the new suburbs ended up with a rather dull, visually boring neighborhood, while the Latino immigrants who poured into the Mission now live in a varied and exciting city district.

The Latino population continues to grow and expand out of the crowded Inner Mission to Bernal Heights and Holly Park, south of Army Street. The lots may be small and the houses built in the slapdash "emergency" style by earthquake refugees using found lunber, but the property is "just barely affordable here, compared to the outlandish prices elsewhere," as one resident commented.

Marc Harrington recently bought "the cheapest house in San Francisco" on Prospect Street in Bernal Heights. He likes the spectacular views of Twin Peaks from his Victorian cottage's windows. Although the neighborhood is 31 percent white, 39 percent Latino, and 12 percent black, Marc doesn't feel any racial tension, although all "the whites seem to live on the view side of the hill." Marc was looking for a "diverse but close neighborhood feeling, not bourgeois, with long-time residents around," and that's just what he's found in Bernal.

But are new residents like Marc actually causing the gentrification they were trying to escape by moving to the heights? *Hills of San Francisco*, a book published in 1959, claimed "Bernal Heights is as unashamedly rural as the outskirts of Petaluma." Grassy hillsides and parks still exist atop Bernal Heights, Holly Park Hill, and in Precita Valley, but the area gets more popular by the year. With increased popularity come higher prices for real estate and more crime.

Bernal Heights and Holly Park, like much of the Mission, were once part of Don Jose de Cornelio Bernal's 4,000-acre land grant. Bernal served as a

Eucalyptus trees screen this public court from Bernal Heights breezes.

soldier in Anza's expedition to the Bay in 1776. He built one of the heights' first structures, a two-story house for his daughter, at the site of Courtland and San Bruno, streets that were laid out after the Civil War. A little flurry of excitement briefly hit the heights in 1876, when Victor Resayre found a tiny bit of gold on the summit, where a microwave antenna stands today.

Nearby Holly Park has been a park since two lawyers gave the land to the city in 1860. This unlikely spot is the home of the first federally funded low-cost housing project built on the West Coast, in 1940. The two hills have always been peopled by working-class folk. More than a third of the residents earn between $4,000 and $10,000 a year. But half of the people here own their homes, and that's what has drawn Marc and all the others to this comfortably ramshackle hill.

EATS AND ARTS IN THE MISSION

Obviously, Mission Street serves as the commercial center for the entire Mission District. In fact, Mission Street is second only to Market as the largest shopping thoroughfare in town. As on Market, a combination of traffic, buses, derelicts, young bloods, and shopping women clog wide Mission.

Snazzy cars not only of interest to Mission males. These women are
driving a car with plush carpeting, custom hubcaps, and a chandelier.

The businesses tend toward bleak discount clothing and furniture emporiums, with a fair sprinkling of Spanish-language movie theaters, markets, and restaurants.

There's nothing really wrong with Mission Street, but to my mind, it just doesn't reflect La Raza the way 24th Street does. The few surprising non-Hispanic establishments on 24th do not detract from the overall Latin American atmosphere.

Go east on 24th from Mission for most of the activity (the block west of Mission holds a popular Angelo cafe, La Boheme, as well as a natural-fruit *paleta*, or popsickle shop, Latin Freeze). First, you

should visit Galeria de la Raza (2855 24th), to get a map of the murals in the neighborhood. I saw a great exhibit of Mexican movie posters there on one visit. Be sure to check out the Balmy Avenue murals just off 24th. Community artists and children painted the walls in 1973. The mural walk ends at the Mexican Museum (1855 Folsom), a gallery that shows contemporary and historic Mexican art.

But the mural walk is a detour. Go back to 24th Street for Mexican food, and try Las Brisas de Acapulco, Roosevelt Tamale Parlor, or Mi Casa—all cheap but good. The St. Francis Candy Store, a pink and white soda fountain from another era, is one of the oddball shops on the street where you'll find a grilled ham and cheese instead of a fried taco.

Two of the best restaurants on the street don't sell a single burrito. El Gallego serves rather elegant Spanish seafood, while Cha Gio's specialty is delicious but inexpensive Vietnamese cuisine (I like the crab curry). There's also an Arab restaurant at 3200 24th Street.

The locals head for La Mexicana, La Victoria, or Dominguez bakeries, to select their own pastries with a pair of tongs and a round tray. Come at Christmas for the anise *bunuelos*. Another local hangout is the barbershop, which has five barber poles out front and a sign that describes the proprietor as "an artista."

If you're looking for Central American food, you must leave 24th. La Olla (2417 Mission) and Nicaragua Restaurant (3015 Mission) both serve excellent Nicaraguan food, while El Salvador is represented well by Coatepeque (2240 Mission) and Aunt Mary's (3122 16th). And there are still a few reminders of the old days in the Mission when Irish and Italians spoke "Missionese"—Dianda Italian Pastry (2860 Mission) and Ireland's 32 Bar (3394 22nd Street).

Two unlikely groups have settled around Valencia Street in the past few years, feminists and punk rockers. The nearby Roxie Theater often shows films that appeal to these groups. Maybe the punks discovered Valencia when they frequented the Club of the Deaf during its heyday in 1978-79. Apparently deaf people could "hear" the hard-driving bass of punk music through the vibrations, so they sponsored live punk rock at their club for dancing. I don't think a surrealist's wildest dream could match the scene at the small upstairs club on Valencia, where half the customers gestured in sign language and the other half pogoed spastically to excruciatingly loud rock.

The police eventually closed down the Deaf Club, but the New Wave lives on in the industrial clothing store, Supplies (3128 16th), where you can buy a nuclear reactor jumpsuit; Valencia Tool and Die (974 Valencia), a showcase for independent film and performance art; and the Photo-Succession Gallery (3321 22nd), exhibitors of such punk photographers as Richard McCaffree and f-Stop Fitzgerald. Other avant-garde but not necessarily New Wave artists perform, live, or exhibit at Project Artaud/Studio Eremos (499 Alabama), Centerspace (2840 Mariposa), Victoria Theater (2961 16th), or Video Free America (442 Shotwell). Regarding the art world, it's hard to draw the line between South of Market and the Mission—both neighborhoods are heavily populated by young artists.

City cowboys of very different sorts frequent a couple of spots in the Mission. Native Americans and Westerners dance to country swing on Friday nights at the Sound Track (Mission at Duboce), while gay cowboys listen to what's advertised as "Shit-kickin' music" at the Rainbow Cattle Co. (Valencia at Duboce).

Lately, jazz clubs with a Latin twist keep popping up in the Mission. Bajones (22nd at Valencia), Kito's (17th and Capp) and Clarion (2118 Mission) all book jazz and salsa bands. But the best club of them all is Cesar's Latin Palace (3140 Mission). Under the glittering ball dangling from the ceiling, Latinos dressed to the nines salsa away to such musicians as Eddie Palmieri. This club's even got a Polaroid camera girl. Cesar's is open after hours, so you can end any evening out on a Latin note in the Mission.

An elusive rebound prompts this energetic pas de deux at
the always-active basketball court in Bayview Park.

11

THE BAYSHORE
PORTOLA • EXCELSIOR • VISITACION VALLEY
CROCKER-AMAZON • BAYVIEW-HUNTERS POINT

MENTION PORTOLA, EXCELSIOR, Visitation Valley, Crocker-Amazon, or Bayview to some San Franciscans and all you'll get is a blank stare and maybe, "Oh, that's somewhere near Daly City, isn't it?" They might have heard of Hunters Point, identifying it with either the shipyards of World War II or the riots of the 1960s, but they almost certainly won't know the term "Bayshore," which the City Planning Department uses to refer collectively to most of these neighborhoods.

The Bayshore is one of those areas that a lot of people go through but not to. Two major freeways, 280 and 101, carry motorists through the Bayshore south to the airport, the Cow Palace exhibition hall, or a Giants game at Candlestick Park. I still remember my first visit to San Francisco when I was twelve years old. As we were riding past Candlestick Park on our way north from the airport, our host informed us that this area didn't "really" count as San Francisco. I

wonder where he thought the thousands of residents here "really" did count?

Actually the Bayshore is a far more stable San Francisco district than some older neighborhoods, such as Haight-Ashbury or Nob Hill, with their transient populations. Single-family homes with neat lawns dominate, about half of them owned by the tenants. But despite a similarity in both appearance and history among the neighborhoods of the Bayshore, the freeway functions almost as a color bar to divide the area into black and white sectors.

Bayview-Hunters Point, to the east of 101, is 66 percent black, which represents the greatest concentration of blacks in the city. Portola, Excelsior, Visitacion Valley, and Crocker-Amazon make up what I call the McLaren Park area. This sector is about 5 percent black, 60 percent white, and 13–29 percent Latino (Visitacion Valley is the exception, with 29 percent of the neighborhood black).

The McLaren Park area surrounds the city's second largest park (after Golden Gate Park), while an abandoned (since 1974) shipyard and a baseball stadium dominate Bayview-Hunters Point. McLaren Park residents have a little more money and a lot less crime than those in Bayview-Hunters Point, but residents of both sides of the freeway are mostly skilled laborers who are struggling with high unemployment.

Like most of San Francisco, the Bayshore was once part of a Spanish land grant. Bayview-Hunters Point, under the name Rancho Rincon de las Salinas y Potrero Viejo (near the salt flats and old pasture), belonged to Jose Bernal in 1834. La Punta de Conca (Seashell Point) became known as Hunters Point after the Hunter Brothers bought the land to develop a town at the time of the Gold Rush.

During the 1860s, William Ralston, director of the California Steam Navigation Company, spent more than $1 million to build a granite drydock at the point that was used until 1916. While oxen hauled stone from Sacramento for the pier, George Hearst attempted to turn the land he owned at Candlestick Point into a fancy residential area, the new Rincon Hill.

But nothing seemed to take hold on the point besides shipping and cattle slaughtering, despite the brief success of a theater, the Bayview Opera House, and the Bayview Racetrack. People never really moved to the area until World War II made Hunters Point the biggest shipyard on the West Coast. The 18,500 employees, many of them black southerners, moved into temporary housing on Hunters Point Ridge. By the time the freeway appeared in 1952, Hunters Point was a black neighborhood composed of rickety temporary houses. The Redevelopment Agency has spent about thirty years replacing the World War II buildings with public housing, a process that's still going on.

Bayview-Hunters Point looks like a place that hit bottom and is slowly starting a change for the better. Beyond the auto wreckers of the old Butchertown, the bulldozers on Hunters Point Ridge, and the barren streets of Bayview are attractive, landscaped housing complexes and Youngblood Coleman Playground, opened in 1979.

The old Victorian Bayview Opera House (47045 Third Street) has been renovated and is run by the Neighborhood Arts Program. Theater productions, classes in dance, photography, and yoga, and a seniors' choir are offered free of charge. Many residents actively participate in the Bayview-Hunters Point Coordinating Council, or Joint Housing Committee. They're working to cut down on the area's biggest problems—crime and unemployment.

Some blacks have moved out of the neighborhood and across the freeway to Portola or Visitacion Valley, especially to the public housing there. Geneva Towers was one of the first integrated projects in the city, although nearby Sunnydale had restrictions against blacks. Lawsuits later struck down the racist requirement, and now Sunnydale is almost all black. Sunnydale is a depressing area of burned-out dwellings, armored stores, and motel-like apartments.

Portola is a much livelier neighborhood, with a busy commercial center along San Bruno Avenue. The old Avenue Theater (2650 San Bruno) shows silent films every Friday to a rather aged crowd. The audience arrives early to sing old songs accompanied by the Wurlitzer organ. There are more beautiful examples of art deco palaces in San Francisco, but none with a more genuine Twenties feel.

Street names around the Portola Recreation Center recall the plan to site City College here years ago. Oxford, Cambridge, Yale, Harvard, and Mt. Holyoke Streets seem out of place in an area where half the residents have less than a high school education.

Portola and Visitacion Valley, like Crocker-Amazon and Excelsior, once had sizable Italian populations. After the earthquake, many Italians and Irish moved out to the rural city around McLaren Park. The park served as a tent city in 1906. Italian delis and restaurants abound here. Caffe Le Botte (1166 Geneva) is a particularly good, informal ristorante in Crocker-Amazon. The latest ethnic group to arrive in Excelsior and Crocker-Amazon are Latinos, moving south from the Mission.

Everybody shops on Excelsior Avenue and Mission Street, the major commercial streets. Although Mission, the older street, displays a few Victorians, both boulevards are overly wide, bare of trees, and singularly ugly, as are many of their side streets.

Right now the Bayshore's major asset, McLaren Park, is under-used and full of arsonists. It certainly is not a draw for outsiders. But would residents want it to be? While there's nothing spectacular about the Bayshore and indeed a lot that's downright ugly, it is a stable area where families can own their own homes. They certainly count as San Franciscans.

12

EUREKA VALLEY • NOE VALLEY

THE TWO VALLEYS that nestle below the protective east slopes of Twin Peaks share the same climate, history, development, and architecture, yet more than just the 22nd Street ridge separates them. Noe Valley maintains a low profile as a friendly family neighborhood while Eureka Valley, like North Beach, is a neighborhood that belongs to the whole city.

Most visitors to Eureka's main drag, Castro Street, don't need very long to figure out the attraction here. Gays from all over the country flock to the Castro. Newspapers from the New York *Times* to the *Village Voice* speculate that the city holds 100,000-200,000 homosexuals, or 20 percent of San Francisco's population. Of course, far from the

whole neighborhood is gay, nor do all city gays live in Eureka Valley (Polk Gulch is an older gay section), but gay men are definitely the most visible group in the Castro.

But the gay influx is a very new phenomenon. Eureka and Noe Valleys spent most of their residential histories as quiet Victorian neighborhoods composed of working-class Germans, Scandinavians, and Irish. The original residents, the Ohlone Indians, roamed the grassy valleys until the Spanish founded the Mission Dolores close by. The Spaniards rounded up the Indians, brought them into the mission village, and sent Candelario Valencia, Francisco Guerrero, and Victor Castro to tend sheep and cattle in the two valleys.

The last Mexican governor of California, Pio Pico, granted Jose de Jesus Noe, the last *alcalde*, or mayor, of Yerba Buena, more than 4,000 acres of land, reaching from Twin Peaks to Daly City, which

Congested shops and the art deco Castro Theatre cluster at the base of the Castro Street hill. Victorian flats atop the hill have fine views of Twin Peaks.

included Eureka and Noe Valleys. Noe's ranch house, at what is now the corner of 22nd Street and Eureka, was one of the first buildings in the district.

Irish and German immigrants moved into the area to dairy farm or work the brickyards at Corona Heights soon after the Gold Rush. By 1890, one-third of the area was covered with Victorians. Lawyer Alfred "Nobby" Clark built a dome-and-tower covered mansion that still stands at 250 Douglass Street. Adolf Scheerer, a German contractor, shipped the materials for his Dolores Heights mansion around the Horn; the decorative statuary came from the old attraction, Woodward's Gardens, a tourist attraction of the 1800s. An adjacent well attracted nineteenth century health nuts to its "miracle water," but was filled in after a woman fell in and miraculously drowned.

Despite the convenience of the Castro Street cable car, installed in 1887, the valleys never attracted many representatives of the upper crust. Noe and Eureka Valleys have remained predominantly middle class right up to the present. The houses are the same wood, two- or three-story Victorians with small yards. Eureka and Noe both escaped the fires of 1906, although Noe houses sustained some earthquake damage due to the softer land there. The Corona Heights brickyards collapsed.

Residents turned out in force to celebrate completion of the Twin Peaks Tunnel in 1917, but the new easy access out to the Sunset eventually contributed to the decline of the valleys after World War II. Noe and Eureka withstood three changes of government, an earthquake, and a depression, but they couldn't compete with the urge for suburban living.

In 1970, Noe and Eureka were sleepy neighborhoods composed of families, students, and office workers, all living in shabby Victorians. Today Noe Valley families are being displaced by young, single professionals. Barbara Hopkins, former president of Friends of Noe Valley, told me, "I feel sad every time I see a house being fixed up, because I know at least four families have been put out." To preserve the "small-town quality where people shop and chat together," the residents are taking a "very hard line on liquor-selling areas. We don't want any more restaurants and bars."

Right now the trendy, redwood-panelled Noe Valley Bar & Grill, Pano's Greek and Seafood Restaurant, Little Italy, and the Acme Cafe, all on the main commercial thoroughfare, 24th Street, draw some outsiders to the neighborhood, as does Small Press Traffic (3841-B 24th Street), an excellent, noncommercial bookstore.

Residents gather at the Meat Market Coffeehouse on 24th Street, or the lovely Renaissance Revival Noe Valley Library (451 Jersey), where the Noe Valley Community Archives are kept. The 24th Street Fair in June is one of the most enjoyable of the city's outdoor block parties. Classic films screen at the Noe Valley Cinema in the Noe Valley Ministry (1021 Sanchez), a "hotspot," according to Barbara Hopkins. Neighborhood information is disseminated through the *Noe Valley Voice*.

Population statistics include both Noe and Eureka Valleys, so it's impossible to know if the extremely high numbers of 25–44 year olds and professionals and managers characterizes both valleys, or mainly Eureka. On a hot fall weekend, the corner of Castro and Market teems with plenty of people who make up the statistics and who spend

Twenty-fourth Street's shops and restaurants draw outsiders to Noe
Valley. Residents are fighting commercialization by limiting businesses
to the street level only and cutting back on liquor licenses.

Gay men are not the only residents of Eureka Valley, but they
are the most visible group along Castro Street.

money freely at the hip and expensive gift and clothing stores all over the neighborhood.

The 2200 and 2300 blocks of Market Street showcase some of the most original and bizarre window displays in the city. I've seen whole storefronts devoted to pig faces, for instance. The Cafe San Marcos, purveyors of a superb chocolate cheesecake and Continental coffee, is in this block. The outdoor Cafe Flore across the street attracts a lot of gay punks. The Patio Cafe, another outdoor restaurant (remember what good weather the Castro has) with a relaxing garden is around back at 531 Castro.

I usually end up in Eureka Valley for one of three reasons: a Reuben sandwich at the New York City Deli (Market at 16th), a movie or a play, or a walk on Corona Heights.

The tiny but high-quality San Francisco Repertory Theater (18th and Collingwood) is just a few blocks from the first nickelodeon built in the area in 1909. SF Rep is particularly fine for Tennessee Williams or Lillian Hellman plays. The Eureka Theater, housed in an old church at 16th and Market, produces new plays. Their midnight shows often feature music. For cabaret, Fanny's (4230 18th) beautiful Victorian is the only place to go. But when you want to see Jean Harlow in *Dinner at 8*, a Cary Grant festival, or the San Francisco Film Festival, it's the Castro Theater (Castro near Market).

Timothy Pfleuger, architect of the exquisite art deco Paramount Theater in Oakland, also designed the Castro Theater in 1922. The theater's interior is all original and in perfect condition, and you get a nostalgic live organ concert on the Wurlitzer before showtime.

Corona Heights, a rough-hewn cliff 510 feet above Castro Street, looks down serenely on the congestion below. The view of the fog slowly billowing over Twin Peaks is without peer in the city. The Josephine Randall Junior Museum is the only structure on the heights. Walk down off the promontory through the hilly residental areas of Levant Street to the Vulcan Stairway. Although San Francisco boasts more than two hundred staircase streets, the most famous being the Greenwich and Filbert Steps of Telegraph Hill, the Vulcan is completely charming. It descends through plum blossoms and rural-style houses with a fine view of the Mission. Here you feel totally removed from the city, although the Market/Castro intersection is right below.

Even during the Gay Freedom Day Parade in June, the Castro Street Fair in August, or the Halloween Costume Parade on Halloween, when thousands of people are attracted to the Castro, Corona Heights and the Vulcan Steps remain quiet and restful. They serve as tranquil retreats from the gay activism and city politics of the Castro (beloved supervisor Harvey Milk, assassinated by Dan White in 1978, was the representative from this district, and his camera store was on Castro Street) or the neighborhood campaigns of Noe Valley. Excitement *and* a quiet retreat—what more could you want from a neighborhood?

Another spectacular view of downtown from a neighborhood hill.
The view point is Buena Vista Park.

13

BUENA VISTA

THE FAITHFUL STILL MAKE the pilgrimage to the most notorious of San Francisco's neighborhoods. You see them standing at the corner of Haight and Ashbury with eyes fixed on the unlikely shrine of the street signs, trying to feel the good vibes left over from the 1967 "Summer of Love." These visitors seem surprised to find a very pretty Victorian neighborhood surrounded by Golden Gate Park, Buena Vista Hill, and the landscaped, sloping yards of substantial houses. The Haight has undergone yet another transformation.

The land now identified as the Buena Vista, which includes Haight-Ashbury, Ashbury Heights, and Upper Market, in the geographic center of the city was once part of the more than 4,000 acres granted to *alcalde* (mayor) Jose de Jesus Noe in the early 1800s. Like most of the city outside downtown, Buena Vista developed in the Victorian age. F. W. M. Lange, a German dairy farmer, built the first house here in 1870, at Cole and Grattan. Governor Henry Huntley Haight, a former San Francisco lawyer, formed a committee in 1870 to create Golden Gate Park. The streets bear the names of the men who brought the park to fruition—Cole, Clayton, Shrader, Stanyan, and Ashbury.

Hammond Hall landscaped the strip of land called the Panhandle that extended from the park through Pope Valley, or today's Haight. The Panhandle looked a lot like Boston's Commonwealth Avenue, except the houses here were wooden Queen Annes, the Victorian style favored in Buena Vista. Like Commonwealth Avenue, the Panhandle became a popular promenade ground for the rich.

By 1890, the Haight was all a proper Victorian neighborhood should have been. It had an elegant promenade, the beginnings of a spectacular park, a couple of neighborhood hill parks with views, a cable car line down Haight Street, the commercial street, to the park entrance at Stanyan, and a breathtaking amusement park named for its waterslide ride, The Chutes.

The wealthy and middle classes quickly built their Queen Annes here (there are more than 1,000 Victorians here) and soon spread up Mt. Sutro and Mt. Olympus. Even the earthquake of 1906 failed to slow development, although it did destroy one popular Victorian retreat—former squatter Thomas U. Sweeney's 1890 observatory, on Strawberry Hill in Golden Gate Park. A few red bricks from the building can still be found around the walk. But basically the Haight escaped damage, and 30,000 refugees moved into tents, and later wooden shacks, in the Panhandle. The tenters even had their own post office there.

Cars and two tunnels finally checked Buena Vista's growth. In 1917, Twin Peaks Tunnel started funneling people out to the Sunset. Eleven years later, the Sunset Tunnel burrowed right under a highlight of the neighborhood, Buena Vista Park, 569 feet high at its peak. Ironically, part of the park had been paved with headstones from old San Francisco cemeteries, but it was the tunnel beneath them that marked the death, however temporary, of the neighborhood.

The decline of Buena Vista continued through the 1950s. The big old Victorians were subdivided into flats, and then divided again. Blacks who had been squeezed out of their Western Addition homes by redevelopment moved west to the Haight and Duboce Triangle. The black population grew from 3 percent of the Haight in 1950 to 50 percent in 1970 (blacks make up 44 percent today).

The Haight had two moments of national notoriety in the Sixties. When the state planned to blast a freeway right through the Panhandle,

residents rallied to fight it off in the Freeway Revolt of 1962. San Francisco became the first American city to kill a proposed freeway. The second Sixties happening was, of course, the brief blossoming of the Flower Children.

Although heroin addiction, violence, and depression followed in the wake of the hippies, the neighborhood was not too demoralized to gather its forces against Mayor Alioto in 1971, when his "Select Committee to Restore the Haight-Ashbury" recommended that everything be torn down. The neighborhood was saved when it was rezoned residential in 1972.

The feisty "Hashberries" who won these victories are still fighting—and winning—neighborhood battles. They pressured the University of California to end their octopus growth on Parnassus Heights in 1975. But now the neighborhood is struggling against a trend, rather than a flesh-and-blood foe like Alioto or the UC Regents. The trend is gentrification, which raises rents and real estate, and thus pushes out blacks, the poor, the old, and families. Perhaps as a left-over of the sixties youth culture, the Haight has more 25–44 year olds than any other city neighborhood.

According to the *San Francisco Perspective*, a community newspaper, a store in the 1300 block of Haight Street was not atypical when it was sold for $46,000 in 1972 and $172,000 in 1978. Calvin Welch, a member of the Haight-Ashbury Council, is concerned about the "astronomical increase in cost of living, speculation and displacement." He's sick of the "yammering about the Mindless Thugs" (see below) he hears from merchants. He'd like to see more community-oriented businesses, such as the Red

Nineteenth century writer Gelett Burgess described Queen Anne houses as
"giving the effect of a nightmare about to explode." But modern San Franciscans
love them and restore them carefully, like these two along the Panhandle.

Victorian Movie House, or a clothes cleaner, than the fern bars and discos going in. "We live in an integrated, central city neighborhood in a beautiful city, and we want to keep it that way."

When Daddy's, a gay restaurant at 422 Haight, opened in 1978, threatening notes and a broken window dramatized the resentment against gays that some residents feel (Daddy's is now closed for

One of the slick new breed of boutiques opening on that old hippie hang-out,
Haight Street. The ugly Sutro Tower is visible in the upper left corner.

unrelated reasons). The former disco, now punk club, I-Beam, at 1748 Haight, is another controversial establishment.

Whether or not the locals like it, the Haight continues to draw visitors to such restaurants as the Ironwood Cafe (Cole and Carl) and The Grand Piano Cafe (1607 Haight), or to the intimate performances at Synergic Theater (545 Haight), Gumption (1563 Page), and the Performance Space (1350 Waller). The clubs offer local comedy (Other Cafe, 100 Carl), jazz

(Cheshire, 1824 Haight), folk (Gorilla Grotto, 775 Frederick), and rock (Le Disque, 1840 Haight). More clubs and shops are opening all the time.

The flatland politics sometimes affect the hill residents too, but you'd never know it by a casual stroll through these well-kept, elegant upper streets. While the tunnels, cars, hippies, and gays changed the neighborhood below, Ashbury Heights remained well-off and well cared for. The area around Java and Masonic Streets is particularly prosperous. The top floor of the Floyd Spreckels mansion (737 Buena Vista Avenue West) once housed the studios of Jack London and Ambrose Bierce, and that's about as Bohemian as the hill people ever got.

A set of stairs at 330 Upper Terrace leads up to a tiny park on Mt. Olympus, a 570-foot hill named for Old Limpus Hanrahan, a crippled milkman (according to legend). The Triumph of Light statue of the Goddess of Liberty that Adolph Sutro placed atop the hill in 1887 was severely vandalized and removed years ago. The next hill to the west shelters one of the prettiest streets around, the brick-paved, plum-lined Edgewood Avenue.

I wondered how much the residents here on the hill knew about the problems of the commercial district down below. A resident out walking on her "morning constitutional" explained, "I do shop there every once in a while, and my children always go to the Haight Street Fair every May. I guess I like to know the Haight's still there, even if I'm not."

THREE-YEAR SUMMER OF LOVE

A popular song of the Sixties gently advised, "If you're going to San Francisco, be sure to wear some flowers in your hair." By 1967, 200,000 young men and women had gone to San Francisco with flowers in their hair and a vision in their heads of a new age of peace and enlightenment.

The media warned parents that their children were "turning on, tuning in, and dropping out" by means of a new psychedelic drug, LSD. The *San Francisco Examiner* dubbed the seekers "hippies," and the rather run-down Victorian neighborhood they crashed in around Haight and Ashbury Streets in San Francisco became famous almost overnight.

Why did the revolution in rock and consciousness grow here, on the Panhandle of the Park? Probably for the same reason that the Beats had earlier settled in North Beach—because it was cheap. A number of the North Beach Beats, such as Allen Ginsberg and Neal Cassady, joined the new Haight movement.

In 1965, Marty Balin, founder of the rock group Jefferson Airplane, opened the Matrix Club; Ken Kesey, author of *One Flew Over the Cuckoo's Nest* and head Merry Prankster, discovered LSD; and Bill Graham produced his first rock concert at the Fillmore Auditorium. Soon afterward, the Psychedelic Shop opened on Haight Street and the Grateful Dead played "acid rock" at the first of the huge rock concerts, the Trips Festival. The Diggers baked bread and scrounged food, which they gave away for free to the people in the streets.

On January 14, 1967, 20,000 tripping people listened to chants, songs, and speeches at the Human Be-In at Golden Gate Park. The Summer of Love was born and everyone wanted in. George Harrison visited the Haight. Margot Fonteyn and Rudolf Nureyev got busted for marijuana at a party in the Haight. Janis Joplin, who lived at 112 Lyon, sang at the Monterey Pop Festival. The other "San Francisco Sound" musicians in the Haight at the time were the

Once the home of the Jefferson Airplane, this huge old house on Fulton Street
now serves as office space for the Jefferson Starship. The Grateful Dead
and Janis Joplin also lived in the Haight in the 1960s.

Grateful Dead (710 Ashbury) and the Airplane (2400 Fulton).

The mood was euphoric, free, and too much fun to escape commercialization. *Vogue* came out with couturier hippie clothes, the "peasant look." LSD became illegal and Gray Line Bus Tours started a "Hippie Hop," so tourists could watch the antics of the strange Haight creatures from the comfort and safety of a bus.

Perhaps the fact that Charles Manson lived at 636 Cole during the Summer of Love was an omen of things to come. By the end of 1967, the Psychedelic Shop had closed down and the Haight dream degenerated into violence and heroin. In 1971, Eugene Block, an old San Francisco newspaperman, angrily wrote in his book, *The Immortal San Franciscans for Whom the Streets Were Named*, "Many now point to the irony of social change that still associates the name of a distinguished lawyer (Henry Huntley Haight) with an area marked by lawlessness, police problems, and judicial burdens."

But the Haight movement didn't die quite so complete or ignominious a death as Block suggests. The Haight Free Clinic still gives free medical attention to all comers. The Diggers have resurfaced for poetry and talk at the "Blabbermouth Nights" held at a classical-music cafe, The Grand Piano (1607 Haight). The Psalms Cafe, the last bastion of Sixties counterculture, is very much in business at 1398 Haight.

In the summer of 1980, a few new manifestoes appeared on the heavily postered walls of the Haight, written by the self-proclaimed "Mindless Thugs." Their tactics (breaking shop windows) were obviously misguided, but their words had a curious air of deja vu: "Remember, you are tolerated only inasmuch as you provide a genuine service for the Haight Community. Street people are part of the community. We resist your attempts to create a bourgeois-clone zone in our neighborhood." After a reward was offered by merchants for information about Mindless Thugs, another poster appeared. "Reward yourself by helping to arrest and eliminate the proliferation of authoritarian and capitalist relationships which paint us into a corner daily and break down our sense of community in the Haight and elsewhere, as well as destroy what little creativity does appear."

Only in the Haight could street anarchists campaign against gentrification in such a blatant way. But many other neighborhood activists are willing to get constructively involved—perhaps exercising a legacy from the Summer of Love.

This ugly sundial at Entrada Court in Ingleside is the western end
of the old Ingleside Racetrack, which closed in 1905.

14

TWIN PEAKS • DIAMOND HEIGHTS POINTS WEST

ST. FRANCIS WOOD • INGLESIDE • OCEAN VIEW MERCED HEIGHTS • WESTWOOD

THE COSTANOAN INDIANS believed the second and third highest hills in San Francisco to be a married couple who quarreled so bitterly that the Great Spirit, tired of their bickering, separated them with a crack of thunder and a bolt of lightning. The Spanish explorers, perhaps on the lonely trail a little too long, called the two hills Los Pechos de la Choca (the Breasts of the Indian Maiden). The Americans unimaginatively changed the name to the simple Twin Peaks.

Mt. Davidson is taller than the peaks, which are 903 and 910 feet high, but the forested Davidson can't match the gorgeous city panorama that Twin Peaks offer. San Franciscans love a view and usually insist on one from their house windows, but even view-crazy San Franciscans left Twin Peaks alone until World War II. The steep slopes, heavy fog, and chilling winds made settlement almost impossible. Architect Daniel Burnham braved the elements for a few months in 1905 while he drew up a new plan for the city, which he overlooked from his high perch.

The most activity Twin Peaks saw in the early part of the century was the hoopla celebrating completion of the reservoir built in 1912. Revelers journeyed up the hills to hear brass bands and speeches. They danced in the empty reservoir ringed by flags. Three years later, the view was preserved for all San Franciscans when the peaks became a park, which itself became easily accessible only after the Twin Peaks Tunnel and Twin Peaks Boulevard were built in 1917.

Berkeley architect Bernard Maybeck designed a few houses here around the time of World War I (196 Twin Peaks is one). Another early structure, the brick

Moffitt house (30 Mountain Spring), took from 1920 to 1940 to complete.

Most of the houses here are Fifties specials, such as the ones at 175-176 Palo Alto and 150 St. Germain. Twin Peaks has its share of bland Fifties apartments, too, especially on the east side, where young singles live. The population here is predominantly white and middle class.

Many of the same kind of people live in the city's newest neighborhood just to the south, Diamond Heights. In 1953, even though almost no one lived in the fog and wind of the heights, the Redevelopment Agency marked the district for renewal, because the existing grid pattern on the steep hill made it impossible to build on. Vernon De Mars laid out a more appropriate contour plan, which produced buildable lots.

Old residents tell a story of Russian smugglers who once hid their contraband in caves on Glen Canyon, the ravine park next door to Diamond Heights, but the tale seems a bit too romantic for this matter-of-fact neighborhood dominated by Eichler homes (a ranch house style developed by an enlightened builder of the 1950s, Joseph Eichler) and high-rise townhouses. An off-beat, wood-and-glass conservatory at 236 Monterey is one of the older buildings in the area. The inventor Frank Merrill built it for himself in 1917.

Twin Peaks, Diamond Heights, Mt. Davidson, and all the neighborhoods to the west and south catch the cold summer fog and wind that race in off the ocean. A lot of people in San Francisco actually like fog and wind, and many of them end up west of Twin Peaks. Even those with big bucks, who could afford to choose a healthier climate, have their own snazzy, but foggy neighborhoods.

Mark Daniels planned out the contoured slopes of one such neighborhood, Forest Hills, in 1915. After the Twin Peaks Tunnel went through in 1917, Bernard Maybeck came in to design houses at 51 Sotelo, 270 Castenada, and 381 Magellan, which is the attractive Forest Hills Club House. Neighborhood volunteers built the club house and gardens, which are rented out for weddings and other celebrations.

The views from Forest Hills feature a bit too much of the Laguna Honda Home, directly to the east, but the pleasant houses and beautiful landscaping make this a very walkable neighborhood.

St. Francis Wood, southwest of Forest Hills, was the original ritzy neighborhood in the southern fog belt, and is the best known. This area, as well as Sherwood Forest next door, was first part of Jose de Jesus Noe's land grant, then a small piece of Adolph Sutro's holdings. St. Francis Wood, along with the Civic Center, is a product of Daniel Burnham's City Beautiful ideas, as interpreted in 1912 by Frederick Law Olmsted, Jr., and John Galen Howard. The entry gate at St. Francis and Portola, the central fountain, the gardens, and the white model Spanish revival houses (44, 50, and 58 San Benito) reflect the aesthetic concerns of the movement.

Unfortunately, the residents of the area didn't believe in an integrated City Beautiful. They kept blacks and Orientals out until their bigoted rules were struck down by the courts in the 1950s.

Now a neighborhood just south of St. Francis Wood and across Ocean Avenue, Ingleside, is almost two-thirds black and 10 percent Latino. Ingleside is an area that the black middle class has moved to. Almost all the houses are single-family structures, three-quarters of them owned by their tenants.

Ingleside's origin goes back to, of all things, the

A craftsman gate opens onto a cloistered garden at this
elegant home of medieval inspiration.

Berkeley architect Bernard Maybeck designed the craftsman-style
Forest Hills Club House. Other Maybeck houses in the neighborhood
are at 51 Sotelo and 270 Castenada.

Ingleside Racetrack. Urbano Drive follows the mile-long loop of the track, which opened in 1885. The land was subdivided years after the track closed in 1905. The biggest and ugliest sundial I've ever seen sits anchored to a green circle at Entrada Court, the west end of the old track. Most of the bigger villa-style houses are on the curved streets near the court.

Ocean View and Merced Heights, two other West of Twin Peaks neighborhoods, are white, middle- and upper-middle-class sections separated by a ridge. As in Ingleside, most of the residents here own their single-family houses, which are nicely maintained if dull. Many of the houses were built after World War II, although developers had made street plans as far back as 1867.

Merced Heights residents once refused to sell lots to blacks and Asians. Today, resident Margaret Dorn mentions the interracial character of the neighborhoods here as an advantage. "Everyone gets along, all races and all classes. We can still afford to buy houses here, although City College and State University students can't find rentals."

All these neighborhoods evolved out of the 12,000 acres that Adolph Sutro owned north and south of Mt. Davidson. Sutro had bought Mt. Davidson itself, the highest hill in San Francisco at 938 feet, from the Noe family. At that time, it was a bald mountain named Blue Hill by geologist George Davidson in 1852. Sutro should have been called "Adolph Eucalyptus Seed" for all the trees he planted on Mt. Davidson (renamed for the geologist in 1911) and elsewhere. The city dedicated twenty-six acres at the top as a park in 1929, even though the trees obscured the view.

Westwood developed only after the forest was substantially cut, a procedure that might have contributed to the hillslide of 1942. One woman died in the thick mud that buried Foerster Street.

While Twin Peaks hosts hordes of sight-seers and walkers, Mt. Davidson is little-used. Only at the Easter sunrise service, celebrated below the 103-foot-tall concrete cross at the summit, do crowds troop up the steep slopes. During the rest of the year, Mt. Davidson surveys the quiet, verdant neighborhoods that completely surround it.

A sunset in the Sunset. A view of the district and the
Pacific Ocean from Sunset Heights on Grand View Peaks.

15

THE SUNSET · LAKE MERCED

MAYA ANGELOU WROTE about the "closed un-dwelled-in-looking dwellings of the Sunset District" in *I Know Why the Caged Bird Sings*. Others joke about the row upon row of identical bungalows built by contractor Henry Doelger, his "White Cliffs of Doelger." Yet in *Pacific Magazine* Supervisor Quentin Kopp called the Sunset "the last bastion of real San Franciscans."

If Kopp means that real San Franciscans are middle class, stable, and long-time residents, he's right about the Sunset. While not as homogeneous a group as in the past (currently three-quarters white, 10 percent Latino, and 5 percent Chinese), the Sunset statistics show a neighborhood where more than half the residents are married and a third are professionals or managers. The Inner Sunset, around the Irving Street commercial district, has more renters and less income than the rest of the neighborhood, but all Sunsetters live without fear of crime in the kind of place "that's ideal for raising kids," as they'll frequently tell you out here.

Who can argue? With Golden Gate Park to the north, Stern Grove, Fleishhacker Zoo, and Lake Merced to the south, and the wide-open ocean (protected by the National Park System, no less) to the west, this is not congested urban living. Of course, that ocean access brings in a treacherous fog all summer, but that "just keeps the shrubbery green," the boosters report.

But if the residents of the "Outlands" are interested in maintaining a small-town quality, a good place to raise kids, and their own detached houses and a garden, why are they living in a city at all? As it happens, the Sunsetters are slowly bringing the advantages of the city—the ones they want—to themselves.

Irving Street, for instance, seems positively international these days. A choice French restaurant

(Le Potiniere, 2305 Irving), a German pastry shop (Heidi's Sunset, 742 Irving), a Spanish eatery with live music (El Bandido, 744 Irving), and an excellent fish grotto (Ernie's Neptune, 1816 Irving) all share the street.

The new Sunset Community Center in the A. P. Giannini School (3151 Ortega) has started to sponsor performances, for instance, those of the Bagong-Diwa Dance Troupe. The clientele at the Avenue Ballroom and Dance Center (603 Taraval) folk dance and jitterbug, or if they feel like Thirties music, they go to the Lost Weekend, an art deco club on Taraval. The Owl and Monkey Cafe (1336 9th Avenue) plays folk and rock music. A fairly substantial Irish community patronizes Finian's Rainbow Bar (48th Avenue) and the theater and music events at the Irish Cultural Center at 2700 45th Avenue (St. Paddy's Day really gets this place moving).

Sunset residents want their entertainment in their own style, on their own neighborhood terms. Other than Irving Street and the recitals at the San Francisco Conservatory of Music, nothing really brings outsiders into the Sunset.

That's been the story of the Sunset right from the start. Until Golden Gate Park began to rise out of the sand dunes in 1870, no one thought living in the Fog Belt south of the park was feasible. In 1887, Arelius E. Buckingham, a speculator, developed land near the streetcar line called "The Sunset," around 5th Avenue and Stanyan.

The next year, Carl G. Larsen, the Danish owner of the Tivoli Cafe on Eddy Street downtown, made enough money selling ham and eggs to the theater crowd to buy land at Golden Gate Heights. He already owned Sunset Heights Park, also called Larsen's Peak. He left both hills to the city at his death. These two areas are the only hill parks with views of the Sunset and ocean in the district.

Development slowly continued, despite the foul weather and miserable transportation. William Crocker's Parkside Realty opened up sites near 21st Avenue and Taraval around 1905.

The Twin Peaks Tunnel, the Sunset Tunnel, and the Judah streetcar line connected the Sunset with the city. Everybody wanted their own homes. In the early 1900s, an eccentric community, Carville, sprang up out of old cable cars retired to the dunes at 48th Avenue and Kirkham, right near the nation's oldest (1926) and the city's only ice rink at 1557 48th Avenue. But builder Frank Doelger knew that the middle class didn't want cable cars, they wanted detached houses with at least a postage stamp of lawn. That's what he gave them. The demand for his almost identical bungalows on 25-foot lots was so great that he sometimes built two in one day, selling them in the 1930s for about $5,000. The clone houses are most prevalent in the mid-thirties avenues.

The Sunset has about 35,000 single-family houses, and they're not all Doelger homes by any means. But even if they were, no one objects to the suburban look. The suburbanization was completed in 1952 when Stonestown, the first edge-of-town shopping center, was built. The whole area still seems very Fifties.

The Parkside section of the Sunset, on the border of the north side of Stern Grove, is a bit more up to date, even though it sports some older, Spanish-style houses. Maybe it's the proximity to Stern Grove that has modernized this section. Free jazz and classical music concerts attract thousands of picnickers every

This gingerbread cottage in Stern Grove was
once a notorious gambling house.

High-rise and low-rise apartments line the convoluted
streets around Lake Merced.

Sunday all summer long. Rosalie Stern donated the grove to the city on John McLaren's advice in 1931. She started the Sunday concert tradition seven years later.

The innocent yellow gingerbread house in the grove was once the Trocadero Inn, a gambling house and hide-out for political shyster Abe Ruef. The two bullet holes in the door date back to the shootout that led to Ruef's capture. Bernard Maybeck wisely left the holes when he renovated the inn in the 1930s.

Another famous shootout had occurred to the south at Lake Merced on September 13, 1859. David Terry, Chief Justice of the California Supreme Court, shot down U.S. Senator David Broderick in a sunrise duel. Broderick, an abolitionist, refused to support proslavery advocate Terry for reelection. Subsequent insults on both sides ended in the fatal duel.

The lake and land had been bought in 1937 by Francisco de Haro for a hundred cows and $25 in goods. Now the neighborhood is mostly water, beaches, a zoo, four golf courses, and San Francisco State University. You can't find a district with fewer people, less public assistance, or a lower percentage of minorities anywhere in the city.

Parkmerced, an overplanned retirement community of low- and high-rise apartments and self-consciously curved streets, was developed by Metropolitan Life in 1948. It helps account for the high number of residents over 60 years of age.

How ironic that a politically active liberal college campus like SFSU sprawls across the most conservative Republican neighborhood in the city, a neighborhood where 61 percent of the residents are married and 31 percent earn $15,000–$25,000 a year.

When SFSU staged a protest strike in 1968 that closed down the school, some Lake Merced residents hoped the school would stay closed for good. It didn't, of course, and Lake Merced residents have learned to accept the university.

One motto San Franciscans understand is, "Live and let live."

INDEX

Alamo Square, 44
Alta Plaza Park, 53
Angelou, Maya, 103
Applegarth, George, 53
Aquatic Park, 19
Art Institute, San Francisco, 33
Ashbury (street named for), 89
Ashbury Heights, 89, 93

Ballet, San Francisco, 36
Banducci, Enrico, 17, 18
Barbary Coast, 14
Bayshore, the, 79-81; Bayview-Hunters Point,
    42, 79, 80; Crocker-Amazon, 74, 79, 81;
    Excelsior, 74, 79, 81; McLaren Park, 79-81;
    Portola, 79, 80, 81; restaurants and bars in,
    81; Sunnydale, 80; theater in, 80; Visitacion
    Valley, 79, 80, 81
Beatniks, 17
Bernal, Don Jose de Cornelio, 74, 80
Bernal, Juan Francisco, 72
Bernal Heights. See Mission, the/Bernal Heights
Bierce, Ambrose, 20, 31, 93
Block, Eugene, 95
Bohemians, 16, 20, 31
Bonzi, Pietro and Orazio, 14
Bookstores: in Eureka Valley/Noe Valley, 84;
    in North Beach, 13, 17, 20; in Richmond,
    59; in Western Addition, 44-45
Brannan, Sam, 3, 55
Broadway strip, 13, 17-18
Brown, Arthur, 16
Buckingham, Arelius E., 104
Buena Vista (district), 89-95; Ashbury Heights,
    89, 93; coffeehouses in, 92, 95; Haight-
    Ashbury, 79, 89-95 passim; Haight and
    Duboce Triangle, 90; nightclubs in, 92;
    Parnassus Heights, 90; restaurants and bars
    in, 92; theater in, 92; Upper Market, 89
Buena Vista Hill, 89
Buena Vista Park, 90
Burnham, Daniel, 36, 97, 98

Caen, Herb, 17, 67
Cameron, Donaldina, 4
Candlestick Park, 74, 79
Cassady, Neal, 17
Castro, Victor, 83
Castro (district), 83
Cathedral of the Holy Virgin, 56
China Basin. See South of Market/Potrero Hill
Chinatown, 1-11; restaurants and bars, 11;
    shopping in, 7-11, 16; a walk in, 7-11
Chinese Cultural Center, 1, 8
Chinese Historical Society, 2, 8
Chinese New Year, 8
Ching, Alex, 2, 3
Civic Auditorium, 36
Civic Center. See Civic Center (district)/
    the Tenderloin
Civic Center (district)/the Tenderloin, 35-39;
    gallery in, 35; named for (Tenderloin), 36;
    restaurants and bars in, 35; theater in, 36
Clark, Alfred "Nobby," 84
Clayton (street named for), 89
Cliff House, 55, 56
Coffeehouses: in Buena Vista, 92, 95; in Eureka
    Valley/Noe Valley, 84, 85; in Marina, 51; in
    North Beach, 20-23; opera in, 20; in Sunset,
    104
Coit, Lillie Hitchcock, 16
Coit Tower, 16
Cole (street named for), 89
Coolbrith, Ina, 31
Coolbrith Park, 32, 33
Corona Heights, 84
Costanoan Indians, 72, 97
Cow Hollow. See Pacific Heights/The Marina/
    Cow Hollow
Crocker, Charles, 26
Crocker, William, 104
Crocker-Amazon. See Bayshore

Daniels, Mark, 56, 98
Davidson, George, 101

Davidson, Mt., 97-101 passim; named for, 101
de Anza, Captain Juan Bautista, 47, 59, 72
de Haro, Francisco, 64, 107
Dewey, John, 31
Diamond Heights. See Twin Peaks/Diamond
    Heights/Points West
Dixon, Maynard, 31
Dobie, Charles Caldwell, 31, 41
Doda, Carol, 17
Doelger, Henry, 103, 104
Dolores Heights, 84
Dolores Park, 74
Duncan, Isadora, 31

Earthquake and fire of 1906, 7, 16, 26, 29, 36,
    42, 48, 62, 67
Eichler, Joseph, 98
Esherick, Joseph, 53, 56
Eureka Valley. See Eureka Valley/Noe Valley
Eureka Valley/Noe Valley, 83-87; bookstores in,
    84; Castro (district), 83; coffeehouses in, 84,
    85; Corona Heights, 84; Dolores Heights, 84;
    restaurants and bars in, 84, 87; shopping in,
    87; theater in, 87; a walk in, 87
Excelsior. See Bayshore
Exploratorium, 50

Fair, James G., 26-27
Ferlinghetti, Lawrence, 17, 20
Filbert and Greenwich steps, 20, 87
Fillmore, the, 41-45 passim
First Russian Christian Church, 64
Fish Alley, 19
Fisherman's Wharf, 13
Flamm, Jerry, 4
Fleishhacker Zoo, 103
Flood, James, 26-27
Flood Mansion, 26
Forest Hills, 98
Fort Mason, 50, 51

Galleries: in Civic Center, 35; in Marina, 51;

in the Mission, 76, 77; in North Beach, 17, 19, 20; South of Market, 62
Ginsberg, Allen, 17
Glen Canyon, 98
Glide Memorial Methodist Church, 39, 61
Golden Gate Heights, 104
Golden Gate Park, 55, 59, 89, 103, 104; the Panhandle, 89, 90; Strawberry Hill, 90
Grace Cathedral, 26, 29
Graham, Bill, 93
Guerrero, Francisco, 83

Haas-Lilienthal House, 48
Haight, Henry Huntley, 89, 95
Haight and Duboce Triangle, 90
Haight-Ashbury. See Buena Vista
Hall, Hammond, 89
Halladie, Andrew, 26
Hammett, Dashiell, 4
Hanrahan, Old Limpus, 93
Hansen, Jay, 41
Harte, Bret, 31
Hayes, Colonel Tom, 36, 44
Hayes Park, 36
Hayes Valley, 36, 44
Hayne, Arthur, 25
Hearst, George, 26, 27, 67, 80
Hearst, William Randolph, 67
Herbst Theater, 36
Herman, Rudolf, 47
Holladay, Samuel W., 48
Holly Park, 74, 75
Hopkins, Barbara, 84
Hopkins, Mark, 26
Howard, H.T., 53
Howard, John Galen, 98
Humphries, William Penn, 30
Huntington, Collis, 26
Huntington Library, 26
Huntington Park, 25, 26
Hyde Street Pier, 13

Ingleside, 98, 101
Inner Sunset, the, 103
Irish Cultural Center, 104

Jackson Square, 14
Japan Center, 44
Japantown, 44
Jones, Jim, 41
Joplin, Janis, 93
Jordan Park, 47
Judah, Theodore, 26

Kearney, Denis, 56
Kerouac, Jack, 17
Kesey, Ken, 93
Kipling, Rudyard, 4
Kopp, Quentin, 103

Lafayette Square, 48
Lake Merced (district). See Sunset, the/Lake Merced
Land's End, 55
Lange, F. W. M., 89
Larkin, Thomas, 47
Larsen, Carl G., 104
Larsen's Peak, 104
Lenoir, Henri, 17, 20
Library, main public, 36
Lincoln Park, 53, 55, 56, 59
Little Chile, 14
Little Osaka, 42
London, Jack, 20, 31, 93
Louise M. Davies Symphony Hall, 35
Low-riders, 71

McElray, William, 48
McKinley Square, 66
McLaren, John, 74, 107
McLaren Park (district), 79-81
Marchant, Grace, 16
Marina. See Pacific Heights/The Marina/Cow Hollow
Marina Green, 50
Maritime State Historic Monument, 13
Maybeck, Bernard, 50, 97, 98, 107
Merced, Lake, 103, 107
Merced Heights, 101
Merrill, Frank, 98
Minority groups, 105; Arabs, 39; Australians, 14; Basques, 13; blacks, 30-31, 37-39, 41-45 passim, 62, 64, 66, 74, 79, 80, 90, 98, 101; Chinese, 107 passim, 13, 16, 26, 59, 98, 101, 103; Eastern Europeans, 44; Filipinos, 44, 59, 62; gays, 29-30, 37-39, 44, 62, 83, 91; Germans, 29, 74, 83, 84; Greeks, 61; Indians, 44; Indochinese, 7, 39; Irish, 14, 26, 59, 61, 64-66, 74, 83, 84; Italians, 13-23 passim, 74, 81; Japanese, 42-43, 59, 62, 98, 101; Jews, 42, 56, 59, 62, 74; Latinos, 59, 62, 64, 66, 71-77 passim, 79, 81, 98, 103; Native Americans, 72, 77, 97; Pathans, 44; Russians, 44, 56, 64; Scandinavians, 44, 74, 83; Scots, 64
Mission, the. See Mission, the/Bernal Heights
Mission, the/Bernal Heights, 71-77, 87; galleries in, 76, 77; Holly Park, 74, 75; nightclubs in, 77; Precita Valley, 74; restaurants and bars in, 72, 76-77; shopping in, 75-76
Mission Creek, 72
Mission Creek Marina, 64
Mission Cultural Center, 72
Mission Delores, 71, 72, 73, 74
Monkey Block, 20
Montandon, Pat, 53
Montgomery, Captain John B., 3
Mooney, Con, 56
Mountain Lake Park, 59
Movies: of San Francisco, 25, 42; foreign language, 8, 44, 76
Murals, 77
Museums, 36, 44, 50, 53, 62, 76
Muybridge, Eadweard, 67

Neutra, Richard, 20
Nightclubs: in Buena Vista, 92; in the Mission, 77; in North Beach, 13, 17, 18-19, 23; in the Sunset, 104; in the Sunset, 104; in Western Addition, 44
Nob Hill. See Nob Hill/Russian Hill
Nob Hill/Russian Hill, 25-33, 67, 79; named for (Nob Hill), 25; named for (Russian Hill), 30; Polk Gulch, 25, 29, 83; Polk Strasse, 29; restaurants and bars in, 29; shopping in, 29
Noe, Jose de Jesus, 72, 83-84, 89, 98
Noe Valley. See Eureka Valley/Noe Valley
Norris, Charles, 31
Norris, Frank, 20
North Beach, 13-23, bookstores in, 13, 17, 20; Coffeehouses in, 20-23; galleries in, 17, 19, 20; named for, 13; nightclubs in, 13, 17, 18-19, 23; restaurants and bars in, 19-23; shopping in, 19; theater in, 23; a walk in, 19-23
Nuestra Senora de Guadaloupe, 16

Ocean Beach, 59
Ocean View, 101
Oelrichs, Tessie, 26
O'Farrell, Jasper, 61
Ohlone Indians, 72, 83
Olmstead, Frederick Law, Jr., 98
Olympus, Mt., 90, 93
Opera, 8, 20, 36

Pacific Heights. See Pacific Heights/the Marina/Cow Hollow

Pacific Heights/the Marina/Cow Hollow, 47-53; galleries in, 51; named for, 47; restaurants and bars in, 51, 53; shopping in, 51-53; theater in, 50, 51
Pacific Union Club, 26
Palace of Fine Arts, 50
Palace of the Legion of Honor, 53
Palou, Padre Francisco, 72
Panama-Pacific Exhibition, 48
Panhandle, the, 89, 90
Parkmerced, 107
Park Presidio. See Richmond, the
Parkside, 104
Parnassus Heights, 90
Peters, Nancy J., 20
Phelan Beach, 56
Pico, Pio, 83
Pleasant, Mary Ellen (Mammy), 42
Polk, Willis, 31, 53, 56, 74
Polk Gulch. See Nob Hill/Russian Hill
Polk Strasse, 29
Portola, Captain Gaspar de, 72
Portola (district). See Bayshore
Portsmouth Square, 4, 8
Potrero Hill. See South of Market/Potrero Hill
Potrero Neighborhood House, 64
Precita Valley, 74
Presidio, the, 50, 51, 56, 59
Presidio Terrace, 56
Prostitution, 4, 14, 36
Publication: concerning San Francisco, 4, 8, 17, 20, 30, 36, 41, 42, 53, 55, 72, 74, 95, 103; in early San Francisco, 3, 4, 48; neighborhood newspapers, 39, 41, 64, 84, 90; poetry, 8, 17; written in San Francisco, 17
Punk rockers, 18-19, 77

Ralston, William, 80
Restaurants. See at individual districts
Richmond, the, 44, 55-59; Presidio Terrace, 56; renamed Park Presidio, 56; restaurants and bars in, 59
Rincon Hill, 25, 26, 61-62, 67-79
Rogers, Mary, 41, 42
Ruef, Abe, 107

Russ, J. C. Christian, 61
Russian Full Gospel Church, 64
Russian Hill. See Nob Hill/Russian Hill

St. Francis Wood, 98
Sts. Peter and Paul Roman Catholic Church, 16
San Francisco Art Institute, 33
San Francisco Ballet, 36
San Francisco Conservatory of Music, 104
San Francisco Museum of Modern Art, 36
San Francisco Opera, 36
Scheerer, Adolph, 84
Sherwood Forest, 98
Shrader (street named for), 89
Silliman, Ron, 39
South of Market. See South of Market/Potrero Hill
South of Market/Potrero Hill, 61-66; China Basin, 62-64, 66; galleries in, 62; restaurants and bars in, 62, 64, 66; shopping in (Potrero Hill), 66; theater in, 62, 64
South Park, 26, 61, 62, 67-79; restaurants and bars in, 67
Spreckels, Adolph, 53
Spring Valley, 47
Stanford, Leland, 26, 27
Stanford University, 26
Stanyon (street named for), 89
Sterling, George, 20, 31,
Stern, Rosalie, 107
Stern Grove, 103, 104-5
Stevenson, Robert Louis, 8, 26
Stewart, Benny, 41
Strawberry Hill, 90
Street People's Park, 61
Sunset, the. See Sunset, the/Lake Merced
Sunset, the/Lake Merced, 103-8; coffeehouses in, 104; the Inner Sunset, 103; nightclubs in, 104; Parkmerced, 107; Parkside, 104; restaurants and bars, 103-4; theater in, 104
Sunset Community Center, 104
Sunset Heights Park, 104
Sunset Tunnel, 90
Sutro, Adolph, 55, 93, 98, 101
Sutro, Mt., 90
Sutro Park, 56, 59

Sweeney, Thomas U., 90
Symphony Hall, Louise M. Davies, 35

Telegraph Hill, 14, 16, 20; named for, 14
Temple Emanue-El, 56
Tenderloin. See Civic Center (district)/the Tenderloin
Tien How Temple, 4
Theater. See at individual districts
Transamerica Pyramid, 20
Transvestite Center, 35
Tucker, J. W. 48
Twain, Mark, 20, 31, 55
Twin Peaks. See Twin Peaks/Diamond Heights/Points West
Twin Peaks/Diamond Heights/Points /West, 74, 83, 97-101; Forest Hills, 98; Ingleside, 98, 101; Merced Heights, 101; Ocean View, 101; St. Francis Wood, 98; Sherwood Forest, 98; Westwood, 101
Twin Peaks Tunnel, 84, 90, 97, 98, 104

Upper Market, 89

Valencia, Candelario, 83
Veterans Auditorium, 36
Visitacion Valley. See Bayshore

Walks: in Chinatown, 7-11, on Corona Heights, 87; in North Beach, 19-23
War Memorial Opera House, 36
Washerwoman's Lagoon, 47
Washington Square, 16
Waverly Place, 4
Western Addition, 41-45, 72; bookstores in, 44-45; Hayes Valley, 36, 44; named for, 42; nightclubs in, 44; theater in, 45
Western Addition Cultural Center, 44
White, Stanford, 29
Whittier Mansion, 48
Williams, Reverend Cecil, 39, 61
Women's businesses, 72
Wurster, William, 53, 56

Yacht Harbor, 48
Yerba Buena (settlement), 3, 64, 83